The Hansard Chronicles

THE HANSARD CHRONICLES

A CELEBRATION OF
THE FIRST HUNDRED YEARS
OF HANSARD IN
CANADA'S PARLIAMENT

John Ward

Deneau and Greenberg

Printed in Canada by John Deyell Company

Canadian Cataloguing in Publication Data

Ward, John, 1927-
   The Hansard chronicles

Includes bibliographical references and index.
ISBN 0-88879-023-6

1. Canada. Parliament. House of Commons. House of Commons debates. 2. Canada. Parliament. House of Commons—Reporters and reporting. I. Title.

JL163.1980W37   070.4'493287102   C80-090036-7

For those who have written shorthand
"in the cause of their country"

Contents

Illustrations

Preface

THIS chronicle has been written to commemorate the centennial of the Canadian House of Commons Debates reporting staff.

Hansard became an official part of the Parliament of Canada on 4 May 1880. Yet the struggle to establish a completely independent, uncensored record of parliamentary debates in Canada began some sixty years earlier. Many of those associated with that struggle suffered grievously, as did their wives and families. The full fury of the Family Compact was vented upon them. They were prosecuted, fined and imprisoned. Some were banished from "the Canadas"; a few were broken in health and in spirit. Newspaper offices were looted, type and printing equipment were destroyed.

While many parliamentarians, historians, students and members of the general public can rhyme off the names of Luke Hansard, William Cobbett, Dr Johnson and Charles Dickens in connection with the establishment and work of *Hansard* at Westminster, few are as fully cognizant of their counterparts in Canada: John Carey, Francis Collins, Ludger Duvernay, Jocelyn Waller, Anthony Holland and Dr Daniel Tracey. These are the forgotten men of Canadian parliamentary history. Their exertions were heroic, the odds against them great. Just how great can be judged from the written comments of one Family Compact supporter, describing Collins as "that precious Scoundrel" and Carey as "that Prince of Liars," jubilant at the treatment afforded Collins in a trial that remains a blot on the Canadian conscience—a trial noted for a packed bench and jury, a twisted verdict and an infamous sentence.

The "precious Scoundrel" and "that Prince of Liars" were the first shorthand parliamentary reporters in Upper Canada. The story of Francis Collins has been told at some length in this chronicle, to recall, for present and future generations, the obstacles placed in the path of those reformers who sought to establish press freedom and true parliamentary democracy in the emerging, independent nation of Canada.

Acknowledgments

T HE compilation of this work was a task made light by the un-
stinting assistance of a number of individuals and institutions.
Foremost in helping with research queries in Canada, Ireland and
the United Kingdom was Lorcan O hUiginn, a former parliamentary reporter in both Ottawa and Dublin. Gerry Duffy of the
Stormont Castle press office in Belfast provided much-needed in-
formation for the story of Francis Collins. Without the Public
Archives of Canada, long-forgotten data might not have been
traced; special thanks are due to the following members of staff:
Miss P. Kennedy, Head of the Pre-Confederation Records; Joyce
M. Banks, Rare Books and Conservation Librarian; Jack Daoust of
the newspaper collection section; Jeanette Cyr of the National
Library; Andrew Rodger, National Photography Collection, and
T.C. Hawkins, Chief, Exhibition Services Division. I also wish to
thank Miss Fernande Desrosiers, Secretary of the Library of St
Paul University, Ottawa; Dympna Murphy, Newry Public Lib-
rary, County Down; the Director and staff of The National Li-
brary of Ireland, in particular Miss Inez Fletcher; J.T. Parkhill,
Director of the Metropolitan Toronto Library; and Mrs E. Jones of
the Fraser Hickson Institute Library in Montreal.

The unfailing courtesy and cooperation of the staff of the
Library of Parliament in Ottawa are gratefully acknowledged.
Many queries were resolved with the assistance of Mike Graham,
Bob le Riche, Don Curtin and Ray Sheehan.

To Rev. J.S. McGivern, S.J., Archdiocesan Archivist, Toronto;
Rev. Brian Price, Diocesan Archivist, Kingston; Rev. Robert J.
Scollard, C.S.B, Archivist, St Michael's College, University of
Toronto; Rev. Robert B. Clune, President of the Catholic Church
Extension Society of Canada; Rev. Gaston Carrière, O.M.I.,
Archivist, Ottawa; and to the Ottawa Jewish Community Centre,

all of whom patiently listened and answered questions, goes a grateful prayer.

The special help so generously afforded by H. Pearson Gundy of Toronto, who placed at my disposal much of his own work relating to *Hansard*, cannot be overly stressed. The kindness of Professor P.B. Waite of Dalhousie University, Halifax, is also gratefully acknowledged, as is that of Miss Shirley B. Elliott, Legislative Librarian, Province House, Halifax.

E.J. Quirk, long-serving member of the House of Commons staff, has been an invaluable reference source because of his personal knowledge of those who have worked on *Hansard* for the past fifty years. Others who assisted were Wilfrid O'Mahony, committee reporting staff, and Charles Fisher of the Ottawa *Hansard*.

For permission to reproduce quotations from other sources, thanks are due to the following:

University of Toronto Press for material from *The Canadian Historical Review*; The Canadian Catholic Historical Association for articles by Rev. Brother Alfred, P.F. Cronin, and Emmet J. Mullally; Messrs Collins, Publishers, London, for an extract from Robert Rhodes James, *An Introduction to the House of Commons*; Messrs Pitman Publishing Limited, London, for a passage from E.H. Butler, *The Story of British Shorthand*; *The Gazette*, Montreal, for E.A. Collard's "Newspaper Scoops"; La Fédération de Quebec des Caisses Populaires Desjardins, Levis, for permission to reproduce material on Alphonse Desjardins.

For permission to reproduce illustrations, I wish to thank:

The National Gallery of Canada ("Cholera Plague at Quebec" by Joseph Légaré); Public Archives of Canada (the *Canadian Freeman*; Francis Collins's petition to Sir John Colborne; Workmen Rebuilding the Peace Tower; Sir John Thompson, age 46; Sir John George Bourinot); La Fédération de Quebec des Caisses Populaires Desjardins (Alphonse Desjardins); Jon Joosten (Charles L. Empringham); Paul Horsdal (Warren Buskard); John Evans Photography Ltd (Edward J. Quirk).

All efforts have been made to locate the owners of copyrighted material. If there are any omissions from the above list, I would be glad to rectify in subsequent editions.

John Ward
Ottawa, January 1980

The *Hansard* Reporter at Question Period

A S the Peace Tower clock chimes to announce the hour, deep within the corridors on Parliament Hill, in the Centre Block, West Block, East Block, Confederation Building—and on the opposite side of Wellington Street, in the Langevin Building and the recently acquired Metropolitan Life office block—other bells, more metallic, but just as insistent, start to jangle. Canada's Parliament, its Chambre des communes, is being summoned into session. The hour is 2 p.m.

Wheeling right, from the Speaker's Corridor into the normally well-crowded Hall of Honour, comes a procession, tiny in numbers, large in tradition. Mr Speaker, his clerks and constables, are proceeding to the Commons Chamber. They are led by the Sergeant-at-Arms bearing the Mace, symbol of the sovereignty of Parliament to conduct its own affairs.

In a corridor one floor above, another procession is under way— in the immortal words of Wodehouse, "a solemn procession of one." There is little solemnity, however. A press of visitors, waiting to gain admission to the Public Gallery, reluctantly gives way. Then a short stairwell must be negotiated, crowded with journalists outside the locked door of the Press Gallery. A long, narrow corridor, crammed with Senate and House guests, diplomats and visiting dignitaries, adds a second figure to the procession, and, eventually, as the last gowntail of the Speaker's retinue passes through the open double-doors of the Commons Chamber, two *Hansard* reporters arrive at the same spot, one to report in English shorthand, the other in French, the debates of the House of Commons, which, when printed, constitute *Hansard*.

Having reached the entrance to the Chamber, the two reporters halt. Mr Speaker takes his place inside, honourable members file into their desks to his right and left, the Mace is placed on the Table in front of him, the stridency of the jangling bells is stopped, and the Speaker begins the ritual of daily prayers, in both official languages. It is a ceremony closed to the public, to the waiting journalists and visitors, and is the one part of the daily proceedings of Canada's Parliament that is not reported by *Hansard*.

When prayers have been said, the bells are rung briefly once more, constables unlock the doors to the galleries, and those waiting take their places in the Public or Ladies Galleries, Senate Gallery, Prime Minister's Gallery, Speaker's Gallery, Members' (East) Gallery, Special Gallery, Members' (West) Gallery, Reserved Gallery, and the Official Gallery. Who goes where is a clue to Ottawa's almost daily changing who's who status. An international ballet star, the President of the Supreme Soviet of the USSR, a new face in the bureaucracy, the 156th Brownie Pack of the Girl Guides of Canada, the two or three regulars in the general public who strive never to miss seeing their favourite politician in action, and the unobtrusive, plain-clothed security officers, scattered strategically amongst them all, take their places. So do the *Hansard* reporters, at desks on the floor of the House, equidistant from the government and the opposition benches.

———

What is *Hansard*? It is the daily record of the legislative history of the country. In its impartial reports, it knows neither parties nor persons. It is consulted by politicians, journalists, historians, teachers, students and librarians, by lawyers, by lobbyists, and by the representatives of foreign countries. Copies of *Hansard* regularly travel by diplomatic pouch to the most far-flung destinations, and its bound volumes are to be found in all major parliamentary libraries.

It is a well-known maxim that those who aspire to a lengthy career in politics must pay close attention to *Hansard*'s treatment of their every speech and interjection (on occasion, the interjections can have equal importance with the actual speeches!).

Let's go down onto the floor of the Chamber and imagine that you are a *Hansard* reporter. You can be either a woman or a man.

You can use a Palantype, stenograph, pen or pencil to write with. But, whichever you use, you must be able to write exceedingly fast, fast enough to present a coherent, free-running, accurate report of what is said within range of your hearing, usually by one honourable member addressing the House, or, in the midst of hubbub, by as many as five—a main speaker and four others engaged in vociferous crossfire. Any *Hansard* reporter worth his salt can handle three, and there are tricks of the trade that can push the number up to five. After that, the noise is generally so loud as to obliterate individual comment; hence the appearance in *Hansard* of "Some hon. Members: Oh, oh!" or "Some hon. Members: Hear, hear!"

On your left, little more than five feet away, sits the Prime Minister. Beside him is the government House leader, and, fore and aft, ministers are ranged along the front row of the treasury benches. On your right, maybe eight feet away—it is a double desk at which you sit—is the Leader of Her Majesty's Loyal Opposition, his House leader, and chief spokesmen. Twist around, and behind you and to your right sit the Leader of the New Democratic Party, his House leader and parliamentary colleagues.

You are a seasoned veteran. You know most of the faces, have heard all their names; indeed, you know without looking the sound of the voices of the most frequent participants in debate. One venerable member has served in the House for thirty-seven years. By now you have a good idea of who is present, or, more precisely, you have noted certain absences. One of them is a member notorious for dropping his voice so low at the end of a sentence that he has always presented difficulty. At least, that is one blessing; the day looks more promising.

Mr Speaker calls the House to order. Until 2.15 p.m. members rise to present motions under Standing Order 43. They make a brief introductory comment, move their motions, and almost invariably are refused permission to place them before the House for debate. It is a daily routine and members show little interest. The House is merely clearing its throat, preparatory to the main event of the afternoon, Question Period. For you as the *Hansard* reporter, the passage is an easy one. Members hand copies of their motions to a *Hansard* messenger; more often than not, the motions are waiting when you return to your office to dictate your notes to an amanu-

ensis, your typist in *Hansard*. (This post has a lengthy and honourable history, dating back many hundreds of years; a *Hansard* amanuensis has duties far more onerous and exacting than mere typing.)

At 2.15 comes the phrase everyone has been awaiting. "Oral
Questions—Questions Orales," Mr Speaker intones, and up pops
the first honourable questioner.

For the next three-quarters of an hour, the proceedings can be
sheer drama. A hot political topic can create a forty-minute
tempest. Questions and answers are hurled, sailed, gently wafted,
sometimes bellowed, sometimes hesitantly proffered, back and
forth across the Chamber. They must be caught by you, now
writing shorthand with intense concentration, and committed to
paper. Names, faces, facts, figures on any subject, must be picked
up by your ear and eye, and instantly sent racing to the tips of your
fingers to spill onto the paper on which you write.

No notice is given of questions to be raised orally. Across the
green-carpeted aisle running down the centre of the Chamber,
members of the government and opposition eye each other's appearance. Who looks tired? Who looks harried? Who gives the appearance of control? Reputations are made, and sometimes lost, on
appearance alone.

Unnoticed, almost a part of the furniture, you, the *Hansard* reporter, are too busy writing to take in all this. But all your senses are
alive. You are testing your skills and experience to their very limits.
And you are interested. You must be, or you simply would not expose yourself to such mental and physical pressure.

Then something intrudes. Did your ear detect a certain hesita-
tion? Mental bells clang. Look out. If it has been detected by the
other side, the pace is going to quicken. It has been. The questioner, sensing it too, "goes for the jugular." Others join in. Go
faster, pen. Keep up at all costs. Where's your relief? Forget it, concentrate, concentrate and write. Mercifully, another minister tries
to divert the attack. It may be the Prime Minister himself. Re-
member, you're writing shorthand. It's not the Right Honourable
Prime Minister you write down every time he opens his mouth.
You use your own shortcuts—PM will suffice. The symbols glide
onto the page of your notebook.

Then, as suddenly as it started, it stops. Mr Speaker steps in,

The Canadian House of Commons Chamber during the mid-1960s. Note the Hansard reporters' desks in the centre of the aisle.

recognizes another member, and you draw a deep breath. "You got it."

To the casual onlooker, it appears effortless. But it is an extremely taxing exercise. Apart from the five-minute period at the beginning of each day, all succeeding "takes" for *Hansard* reporters are ten minutes long: ten minutes to write, and fifty minutes to dictate what you have written. It doesn't seem like much, but those ten minutes are such concentrated work that few who try it can successfully cope with it on a daily, weekly and monthly basis.

When transcribing each sentence or utterance, the reporter must decide on structure, grammar and sense. Particularly when polishing a member's speech for publication, one delivered extemporaneously and without notes, the reporter must retain the personal idiomatic flavour of the member speaking, but within the framework of accepted grammatical usage. *Hansard* serves both the institution and the individual. In its own way it tries to uphold the dignity of Parliament, and has a proven record of success.

The *Hansard* reporter's life is largely dictated by the tintinnabulation of bells. In the *Hansard* office there is an electric clock that every ten minutes rings a warning bell, whereupon one reporter will lift his notebook or writing machine and begin the procession to the Chamber. It is a two-minute walk, no more, no less. The reporter's colleague who is on the floor, on occasion "writing like crazy," has a built-in human timepiece. Let his successor be ten seconds late and he is made aware of it, sometimes in quite unparliamentary language, of which Mr Speaker, and parliamentary authorities, Beauchesne and Bourinot, separately and conjointly, would not approve.

The happiest bells to a reporter's ears are the division bells. Almost every time a recorded vote is required in the House, Mr Speaker "calls in the members." His way of doing so is to have an uninterrupted ringing of the bells take place until the agreed-upon time for the taking of the vote, or until the various party whips are satisfied that all their available members have arrived in the Chamber. During this period no business is conducted, and there is nothing to report. Happy is he or she whose "take" is reduced to the simple notation "Take in Division."

The actual counting of the members is done by clerks at the

Table. As each member rises in his place, his name is called out by one official, and repeated and checked by others who do the actual counting. Within a few seconds of the last member rising, the final tally is announced. It is a peculiarly Canadian procedure. Elsewhere, in many other national assemblies, members leave their places and pass through "Yea" and "Nay" lobbies—centrally located desks at which official tellers and clerks sit, the tellers themselves being members working in an honorary capacity.

Considering that, on average, a third of the membership of the House changes at each general election, instant recognition of new names and faces for the first crucial vote in the succeeding Parliament is a nerve-wracking duty for the clerk charged with the task of calling out the names of all members. In recent decades the late Gordon Dubroy was a master of the art.

At the end of each day's Question Period, the House of Commons usually begins debate on legislation proposed by the government. Members speak in both French and English, and are reported in whichever tongue they use. For as long as the House sits, the reporters take turns on the floor. The normal day draws to a close at 10.30 p.m., and the reporter who has had the last "take" will leave for home before midnight.

One difference between the Ottawa and Westminster *Hansard* reporters has to do with their physical location when they are working. At Westminster they work from a gallery overlooking the Chamber and, in consequence, have two reporters writing simultaneously, to assist each other in recognizing members and in catching interjections. Ottawa, Dublin and other national legislatures have the more practical system of seating their reporters on the floor of the House. Those who first devised and sanctioned the Canadian system did a good job.

Behind the public manifestation of *Hansard*, there is also the internal operation. Many people may have heard the word "blues" in connection with *Hansard*. Few know that there are also "whites," "greens," and "yellows." The old London street cry, "Penny plain, tuppence coloured," could well be applied in reverse. The "whites" are the final edited copy which is sent at intervals during the afternoon and night to the printers, for publication and distribution next morning as the daily issue of *Hansard*. "Yellows" are the reporters' copy from the French debates office, which must be interleaved correctly and in proper sequence with the "whites." The "greens'" are the English reporters' copy which is immediately forwarded to the members of the Press Gallery as soon as dictated and printed in sufficient volume in *Hansard*'s own print shop. Then there are the "blues." They are carbon paper copies of the "greens," and have a certain status associated with them.

Only cabinet ministers, parliamentary secretaries and ex-cabinet ministers receive "blues" after speaking in the House. They may correct gross errors in the transcript, but may not alter the meaning of what they uttered.

As "takes" are transcribed, the "whites" are edited by a trio of editors, working in shifts, the last of whom may not vacate the premises until well into the early hours of the following morning.

Another part of the operation, hidden from public view, is the work of the translators. All members' speeches are reported and transcribed in the language in which they are delivered. Then they are translated into the other official language.

There are two separate daily issues of *Hansard*, one in English, one in French. The work of translation and of printing also goes on through the day and night in order that both issues may be available early next morning.

Such is a working day in the lives of *Hansard* reporters. They write shorthand in the cause of their country. And the genesis of their being is a fascinating, occasionally exciting, story.

William Cobbett—Ploughboy and Patriot

T HROUGHOUT the story of Francis Collins, at almost every turn in the chronicling of *Hansard*, and singularly at the forefront of the reporting of debates at Westminster, William Cobbett's name reappears. His influence is all-pervasive. From his pen flowed reform of parliament, universal suffrage and freedom of the press. Cobbett became the conscience of a nation. During his lifetime he saw the last gasp of feudalism and the foundation of parliamentary democracy in his own country, and he played a telling role in testing the limits of infant democracy in the United States.

Thomas D'Arcy McGee, one of the Fathers of Confederation, summed up Cobbett's work as follows: "There was more strength in his pen than all the reviewers of the land could muster, and his facts were as inexhaustible as his logic was vivid."* McGee wrote this in 1845, ten years after Cobbett's death, which follows neatly the dictum of the British MP Charles Pannell, spoken in Ottawa on 30 September 1966: "We have a good rule in parliament by which you never celebrate a man within ten years of his lifetime because you are too near the mountain." Cobbett and his works constitute a veritable mountain.

Some mystery surrounds the date of Cobbett's birth, it being given variously as 6 March 1763, 9 March of the same year, and also 9 March 1762. He himself said that he had been born in 1766. However, there is no mystery concerning his parents. His father farmed on the outskirts of Farnham in Surrey. His grandfather had been a farm labourer who "worked for one farmer from the day of his marriage to that of his death, upwards of forty years."

*In *Historical Sketches of O'Connell and Friends* (Boston: Donahoe and Rohan, 1845), p. 94.

William was the third of four boys, all of whom went to work on the family farm. He has left us a vivid picture of his early days:

> A father like ours, it will be readily supposed, did not suffer us to eat the bread of idleness. I do not remember the time when I did not earn my living. My first occupation was driving the small birds from the turnip seed, and the rooks from the peas. When I first trudged afield, with my wooden bottle and my satchel swung over my shoulders, I was hardly able to climb the gates and stiles, and, at the close of the day, to reach home was a task of infinite difficulty. My next employment was weeding wheat, and leading a single horse at harrowing barley. Hoeing peas followed, and hence I arrived at the honour of joining the reapers in harvest, driving the team and holding plough. We were all of us strong and laborious, and my father used to boast that he had four boys, the eldest of whom was but fifteen years old, who did as much work as any three men in the parish of Farnham. Honest pride, and happy days!*

This is a picture of life almost two hundred years ago. Who could then foretell that the boy behind the plough was to become, among other things, the original compiler of parliamentary debates as we know them today? And who could foretell that in Ottawa today there lives a direct descendant of the Cobbett tradition, a man who has spent most of his adult life producing parliamentary committee reports for the Parliament of Canada, and who, too, has vivid memories of handling a team of plough horses when growing up on his father's farm near Simcoe, Ontario? Wilfrid O'Mahony is that man, and it has been an honour to have had his assistance in compiling this book.

The young Cobbett had little formal schooling, as he acknowledges in *The Life and Adventures of Peter Porcupine:*

> In the winter evenings my father learnt us all to read and write, and gave us a pretty tolerable knowledge of arithmetic. Grammar he did not perfectly understand himself, and therefore his endeavours to learn us that, necessarily failed; for, though he thought he understood it, and though he made us get the rules by heart, we learnt nothing at all of the principles.

*The passage is taken from *The Life and Adventures of Peter Porcupine*, Cobbett's autobiography, published when he was thirty-three and living in the United States.

Thus did Cobbett spend his boyhood until the age of eleven years, when an event that was to determine his destiny occurred. He read a book. But not any book.

A long day (it was in June) brought me to Richmond in the afternoon. Two pennyworth of bread and cheese and a pennyworth of small beer, which I had on the road, and one halfpenny that I had lost somehow or other, left threepence in my pocket. With this for my whole fortune, I was trudging through Richmond, in my blue smock-frock and my red garters tied under my knees, when, staring about me, my eye fell upon a little book in a bookseller's window, on the outside of which was written: TALE OF A TUB; price 3d. The title was so odd, that my curiosity was excited. I had the threepence, but, then, I could have *no supper*. In I went, and got the little book, which I was so impatient to read, that I got over into a field, at the upper corner of Kew Gardens, where there stood a *hay-stack*. On the shady side of this, I sat down to read. The book was so different from anything that I had ever read before: it was something so *new* to my mind, that, though I could not at all understand some of it, it delighted me beyond description; and it produced what I have always considered a sort of birth of intellect. I read on till it was dark, without any thought about supper or bed. When I could see no longer, I put my little book in my pocket, and tumbled down by the side of the stack, where I slept till the birds in Kew Gardens awakened me in the morning; when I started to Kew, reading my little book.*

The impact of Jonathan Swift on the mind of the eleven-year-old boy was cataclysmic. The little threepenny book became his most precious possession, "which I carried about with me wherever I went, and when I, at about twenty years old, lost it in a box that fell overboard in the Bay of Fundy in North America, the loss gave me greater pain than I have ever felt at losing thousands of pounds."

In London, in 1783, employed as a "quill-driver," or clerk, to one Holland, an attorney in Gray's Inn, Cobbett sharpened his rustic penmanship skills. But not finding the closed and closeted

*Edward Smith, *William Cobbett*, Vol. I (London: Sampson, Low, Marston, Searle & Rivington, 1878), pp. 14-15.

atmosphere of a lawyer's office to his taste—the most dismal nine months of his life—he resolved to join the marines and see the world. By mistake he joined the army instead, the 54th Foot, Chatham division, in which he was to serve upwards of eight years, most of them in New Brunswick.

Cobbett's first impressions of Halifax, Nova Scotia, where he joined his regiment in 1785, were not particularly pleasant:

> Thousands of captains and colonels without soldiers, and of 'squires without stockings or shoes. In England I had never thought of approaching a 'squire without a most respectful bow; but, in this new world, though I was but a corporal, I often ordered a 'squire to bring me a glass of grog, and even to take care of my knapsack.

After a few weeks stay in Nova Scotia, Cobbett and his regiment were ordered to New Brunswick.

His years of service were marked by an overriding determination to better his lot in life. Even before reaching Canada, he had become a corporal, and before he left New Brunswick had risen to the rank of regimental sergeant-major. All the while he studied and read, making himself indispensable to his superiors, so much so that some of his work came to the attention of the Lieutenant-Governor of the province, General Carleton, afterwards Baron Dorchester, Governor-General of Canada.

While working and studying at Fredericton, Cobbett grew disenchanted with army life, and particularly with the corruption rampant in the 54th. The ordinary soldier was made to suffer more grievous hardship and privation than was the normal lot of the lower ranks of the day. Cobbett discovered that the quartermaster kept about a fourth of the men's provisions to himself, and that other officers profited from the illegal sale of supplies. He complained: " . . . the reception I met with convinced me, that I must never make another complaint till I got safe to England, and safe out of the reach of that most curious of courts, a *Court-Martial*." To that end, Cobbett set about copying regimental records, detailing offence after offence. He was helped by a Corporal Bestland. The material they amassed was to form the basis of charges Cobbett would lay when both were safely out of the army and home in England.

It was in New Brunswick that Cobbett met his future wife, Ann Reid, who was just thirteen when they got to know each other. Her father was also a sergeant, but in another regiment. Cobbett himself was about twenty-four years old. His suit quickly found favour, and they were soon engaged. However, within the space of a year, Ann, her father and his regiment all moved back to England, and Cobbett soldiered on in New Brunswick, a bachelor, until the 54th Regiment returned home in 1791.

On 19 December 1791 Cobbett received his discharge from the army. Twenty-six days later, he wrote a letter to the Secretary at War, Sir George Young, charging three of his former officers with misuse of funds. On 24 January, he was called for an interview with Young. (On 5 February, he was married to Ann Reid.) On 15 February, having again pressed the matter with Young, he was informed that a court-martial would be held at Portsmouth. Given Cobbett's knowledge of courts-martial, this was the last place he could expect a fair hearing. He appealed to Pitt, the Prime Minister, and the venue was changed to London. Then the authorities began to drag their feet; production of the regimental records was postponed time and again. Worse still, poor Corporal Bestland, whose ties with Cobbett became known, was refused his discharge.

Cobbett recognized the signs well. His own financial resources, made up solely of savings from his army pay, were being eaten up. Not only for his own sake but for his friend, Bestland's, he decided to cut his losses. England was not yet ready for Cobbett the reformer. After writing to Young on 20 March, Cobbett left for France. A few days later the court-martial was convened and, in Cobbett's absence, the three defendants were acquitted. One might say it was a bureaucratic win, but, as events unfolded, it became a costly pyrrhic victory. Cobbett had taken his measure of important people in places of power, and in later life used the knowledge he had gained to further the cause of democracy and hasten the demise of undeserved privilege.

After five months in France, Cobbett sailed to America, arriving in Philadelphia in October 1792, where he taught English to the many French emigrés who had made the city their adopted home. He spent the greater part of the next eight years there and became a pamphleteer, publisher, author, and, in 1796, made his first contact with parliamentary reporting when he issued *The Prospect from the Congress Gallery.*

> I proposed making a mere collection of the debates, with here and there a note by way of remarks . . . When about half a Number [i.e. issue] was finished, I was informed that many gentlemen had expressed their desire that the work might contain a good deal of original matter, and few debates. In consequence of this, I was requested to alter my plan; I said I would, but that I would by no means undertake to continue the work.

Here Cobbett was displaying his growing sense of independence. Pressured to write what others wanted, not what he himself had planned, he explodes:

> What! A bookseller undertake to promise that I should write, and that I should write to please his customers too! No; if all his *customers*, if all the Congress with the President at their head, had come and solicited me; nay, had my salvation depended on a compliance, I would not have written another line.

He promptly changed publishers for the second issue, and continued as he had originally intended. However, he was obliged to change the title, which now became *The Political Censor.* It was controversial and a great success. By the time Cobbett eventually returned a second time to his homeland (8 July 1800), he was an accomplished craftsman, a satirist who knew how to marshal facts and pound them, mercilessly and without cease, into the consciences of his fellowmen, until redress was secured or the aristocratic supporters of the status quo were goaded into retaliation.

Having fled his homeland because of the risk of court-martial, Cobbett might have been expected to embrace Yankee republicanism without much enticement. Instead, he became the most noted supporter of England to be found in the twenty-year-old United States of America, much to the displeasure of France and her supporters in Philadelphia and elsewhere, so much so that his published defences of England's case were reprinted by the authorities in London and given widespread distribution.

His energy was seemingly limitless. In March 1797, he founded a daily newspaper, *Porcupine's Gazette and Daily Advertiser*, and, as a presage of things to come, was twice charged with libel. In the first case, instituted at the behest of the Spanish ambassador, the grand jury, by a majority of one, threw out the indictment. Incidentally, the then Chief Justice, Thomas McKean, was father-in-law of the Spanish diplomat, and did not take kindly to this result. Two years later a Republican physician, Dr Benjamin Rush, sued Cobbett's *Gazette* for libel, a case which took two years to bring to trial. With his earlier experience of the postponed court-martial to guide him, Cobbett well knew the reason for the delay, and how the judicial land lay. By the end of the two-year period he had removed his bookselling business to New York, and contrived to leave as little of his material possessions as he could in Philadelphia. It was a prudent precaution. The eventual sentence gave the physician $5,000 in damages. Cobbett's Philadelphia assets were speedily seized and sold, but realized little. In fact, the balance of the $5,000 was raised by voluntary subscription.

Cobbett moved to New York following this trial in 1799, and on 1 June 1800 set sail once more for his homeland.

He was now approaching his fortieth year. His defence of his country's policies, while he was in the United States, had earned him the gratitude of Pitt's administration, which now offered him his choice of two government-controlled papers. He declined, wishing to keep his independence. After dabbling in a number of ventures, he resolved to establish a journal tailored to his own plans. The famous *Political Register* made its appearance on 16 January 1802. It was with this newspaper that the erstwhile ploughboy was to make his mark over the next thirty-three years, and leave a legacy of courage to free men all over the globe.

Edward Smith, in his biography of Cobbett, had this to say about the venture:

It is very easy to understand and account for the immediate success of the *Political Register*. The plan had long been in Cobbett's mind. It partook of the qualities of his Philadelphia *Censor*, joined to those of a weekly newspaper: parliamentary debates, public official documents, foreign intelligence, weekly prices-current, and diary of the weather, &c., along with the editor's summary of politics, made up such a journal as was wanted—not only for periodical instruction, but that might furnish a ready means of reference. As projected and as carried out for the first two years, the *Register* was far in advance of anything that had been hitherto attempted. About three hundred subscribers were found, to start with, the price being 10d. per number, fortnightly. But the two numbers for January were so far successful, that February 6th saw the commencement of a weekly issue.*

Cobbett's development as a reformer can be easily traced through the columns of the *Political Register*. In 1816 his influence expanded enormously with the publication of a cheap edition of the *Register*. Priced at only twopence, it quickly reached a circulation of more than 40,000 copies per week. By now, parliamentary reform was the clarion cry, and its benefits were described by Cobbett in the *Register*:

(1) It would do away with the profligacy, bribery, and perjury of elections. (2) A Reformed Parliament would instantly put an end to that accursed thing called *Parliamentary Interest* and open the way to the appointment of persons to posts of trust by merit. Thus would the nation be sure to have the full benefit of all that it needed of the best talents and greatest virtues that it possessed. (3) A Reformed Parliament would, in the space of one single week, examine the long lists of Sinecures, Pensions, Grants, and other emoluments of individuals derived from the public purse . . . (4) A Reformed Parliament would, without a day's delay, set a Committee to work to inquire into the amount of the *salaries* of all persons in public employ . . . (5) It would reduce the Army, and sift the Navy, taking the same care to do justice to the lower ranks. (6) A Reformed Parliament would . . . want no *secret service money*: it would sweep away the hosts of "horrid scoundrels" and informers; . . . (7) It would reform the Bar, by relieving it from its subservience to ministerial interests. (8) It would restore real freedom to the press, and give up all forms of influencing and subsidising the newspapers . . . (9) It would dras-

*ibid., pp. 284-85.

tically cut down the Civil List and reform the administration of Crown lands . . . . *

Cobbett also called for reform of the voting system. His prescription was strong medicine, and he was branded an out-and-out radical. To this he replied: "A thousand times over have I said that we wanted *nothing new*. I say so still. We want the laws of England. We want to destroy neither Kings, Nobles, nor Church. We want the laws of England, and *the laws of England we will have*."

The *Political Register* was not destined to escape for long the inevitable ministerial retaliation. In 1804 the first blow was delivered.

Some anonymous Irishman, signing himself "*Juverna*," had, in November of 1803, immediately after Robert Emmet was executed, published a series of letters in Cobbett's *Political Register*, containing severe animadversions upon Lord Redesdale, Lord Hardwicke and his government, upon the public proceedings of Secretaries Wickham and Marsden, upon a charge delivered by Mr Justice Osborne, and other matters. No government in Ireland ever before had the press so thoroughly corrupted or intimidated as that of Lord Hardwicke; and the first of the "*Juverna*" letters was sent to Mr Cobbett avowedly because every printer in Dublin had refused to publish it. The sturdy William Cobbett (who was then, and for many years after, a sharp thorn in the side of Pitt and Castlereagh) admitted the letter at once to his *Register*; and then several others. These letters excited much attention, and extremely exasperated the Government, because they were evidently the production of some personage highly placed, who knew the secret machinations of the Irish officials against the people.

Great efforts were made to discover the audacious "*Juverna*;" but in the meantime, as the next best thing, the Attorney-General prosecuted Cobbett himself for publishing the "libels." His trial took place on May 24, 1804.

Cobbett had an interval of repose from persecution of *two days* allowed him, when, at the suit of the Right Honourable W.C. Plunket, Solicitor-General of Ireland, he was again called on to sustain an action for libels contained in letters signed "*Juverna*," published in the *Register*, reflecting on Mr Plunket's conduct on the

Political Register, 12 October 1816.

occasion of Robert Emmet's trial. Cobbett was again convicted, and damages were awarded to the plaintiff to the amount of £500.*

Worse was to follow. Cobbett was prosecuted again in 1810 in the Court of King's Bench, on an indictment charging him with seditious libel. The sentence, pronounced on 5 July, was severe: two years' imprisonment in Newgate jail, a fine of £1,000, and bail in the amount of £3,000, with two sureties of £1,000 each, to see that he "kept the peace" for seven years. For the next nine years Cobbett worked under severe restraint. Something of the real mettle of the man is revealed when, at the end of his two years in Newgate, he wrote that he had "just paid a thousand pounds to the king: and much good may it do his majesty!"

In 1817 the Habeas Corpus Act was suspended, rendering Cobbett liable to reimprisonment at any time, without notice, and he had to flee his homeland once more. It was back to the United States, where this time he settled on a farm on Long Island, not far from New York. Incredibly, except for the time occupied by his journey to safety, he continued to publish the *Political Register*.

The year 1819 saw Cobbett's third return to England. Except for a visit to Ireland in 1834, he never went abroad again. Yet the establishment did not leave him alone in his last years. One more attempt was made to crush him. In July 1831, again in the Court of King's Bench, he appeared on an indictment for "a libel, with the intent to raise discontent in the minds of the labourers in husbandry, and to incite them to acts of violence, and to destroy cornstacks, machinery, and other property." But the times were changing, and not even a packed jury, after deliberating all night, could find it in them to bring in a verdict of guilty.

News of the trial reached Canada two months later and was reported in the *Canadian Freeman* of 15 September:

Cobbett has been tried for an alleged libel, tending to excite the farming laborers to destroy threshing machines, &c. The jury could not agree, and were discharged. Cobbett claims this as an acquittance.

*John Mitchel, *History of Ireland*, Vol. II. (Glasgow: Cameron, Ferguson & Company).

An acquittance it was. It was the last great political persecution of the press in England, and signalled the approaching end of similar oppression in dominions overseas. *If* there is freedom of the press today in Canada, it is due in no small measure to William Cobbett, Francis Collins, Ludger Duvernay, and to other courageous men who endured prison, fine and exile so that their colleagues and descendants might live as truly free men and women.

At the time of this last trial Cobbett was seventy years of age. He defended himself, and his address to the court lasted several hours. It was an outstanding performance. Castigating his enemies, he declared:

I have been writing for thirty years, and only twice out of that long period have I been brought before this court. The first time was by an apostate Whig. What, indeed, of evil have the Whigs not done? . . . It was they who seized what remained of the Crown lands; it was they who took to themselves the last portion of Church property; it was they who passed the monstrous Riot Act; it was they also passed the Septennial Bill . . . Then came the excise laws which were brought in by the Whigs; and from them, too, emanated that offensive statute by which Irish men and women may be transported without judge or jury. There is, indeed, no faction so severe and cruel; they do everything by force and violence: the Whigs are the Rehoboam of England; the Tories ruled us with rods, but the Whigs scourge us with scorpions!

The last time I was brought before this court, I was sent out of it to two years' imprisonment among felons, and was condemned to pay, at the expiration of the two years, a fine of £1,000 to the King, which the King took and kept . . . For what was it that I was condemned to this horrible punishment? Simply for writing a paragraph in which I expressed the indignation I felt at an English local militiaman having been flogged under a guard of German bayonets! I only expressed the indignation I felt, and I should have been a base creature indeed, if I had not expressed it. But now, military flogging incites universal indignation . . . But why am I tossed down before this court by the Attorney-General? What are my sins? I have called on the Government to respect the law; I have cautioned them that hard-hearted proceedings are driving the labourers to despair; that is my crime . . . The ministry, however, will perhaps adopt the measures I have recommended, and then prosecute me for recommending them. Just so it is with parliamentary reform, a measure which I have been foremost in recommending for twenty years. I have pointed out, and insisted upon, the sort of reform that we must have; and they are compelled already to adopt a large part of my suggestions, and avowedly against their will. They hate me for this; they look upon it as I do, that they are married to Reform, and that I am the man who has furnished the halter in which they are led to church. For supplying that halter they have made this attack on me through the Attorney-General, and will slay me if they can. The Whigs know that my intention was not bad. This is a mere pretence to inflict pecuniary ruin on me, or cause me to die of sickness in a gaol; so that they may get rid of me, because they can neither buy nor silence me. It is their fears which make them attack me, and it is my death they intend. In that object they will be defeated; for, thank heaven, you stand between me and destruction. If, however, your verdict should be—which I do not anticipate—one that will consign me to death, by sending me to a loathsome dungeon, I will with my last breath pray to God to bless my country and curse the Whigs; and I bequeath my revenge to my children and the labourers of England.*

Four years later, on 18 June 1835, William Cobbett breathed his last.

*Edward Smith, *William Cobbett*, Vol. II, pp. 271-74.

Cobbett and *Hansard*

REFERENCE to the connection between Cobbett and *Hansard* was deliberately omitted from the preceding chapter. A brief mention was made of Cobbett originating *The Prospect from the Congress Gallery*, later *The Political Censor*, in Philadelphia in 1796. Seven years afterwards, on 3 December 1803, he began publishing its natural successor in London, *Cobbett's Parliamentary Debates*, at a price of one shilling. It was issued as a supplement to his weekly *Political Register*, and was the first issue of what is universally known today as *Hansard*.

> This undertaking has long since made the name of Hansard famous; but this is the place to remind the reader, that its origin, and successful issue for a number of years, is one of the long-forgotten public services of William Cobbett. The original form is still retained.*

To superintend the task, Cobbett appointed as reporter and editor John Wright, an anti-Jacobin bookseller, who had gone through bankruptcy—according to Cobbett the consequence of taking more delight in reading books than in selling them. "Seeing him once more ready to begin the world afresh, I proposed to him the editing of the parliamentary debates, of which we have now [1810] continued the publication since the year 1803." Mr Wright became a friend of the Cobbett family, but unfortunately his business acumen remained sadly deficient.

In addition to his current *Parliamentary Debates*, in 1806 Cobbett undertook another monumental task: compiling a full report of any and all recorded proceedings in the English parliament "from

*ibid., Vol. I, p. 310n.

21

the earliest times to 1803," and again entrusted Wright to oversee the assignment. The latter farmed out the work, paying with a liberality that was to cost his employer dearly. In all, sixteen volumes of Cobbett's *Parliamentary History of England* were produced. It was the first really successful attempt to collate various fragments of parliamentary debates dealing with the period following the Norman conquest onward, that had survived in odd collections of print and manuscript.

In 1809 an event of some significance took place. Cobbett changed printers. The firm of Cox and Baylis was replaced by Thomas Curzon Hansard, a son of Luke Hansard, who had earlier procured the contract to print the *Journals* of the House of Commons. A year later Cobbett was prosecuted in the Court of King's Bench, as has already been described, and received a savage sentence. His printer, Hansard, who had been charged with him, was sentenced to three months' imprisonment.

While Cobbett was in jail, his financial affairs came a cropper, thanks in some measure to Wright, and he divested himself of his proprietorship of both the *Parliamentary Debates* and the *Parliamentary History*, which passed into the hands of Hansard in 1812. Thus *Cobbett's Parliamentary Debates* became *Hansard's Parliamentary Debates*, abbreviated over time to the now familiar *Hansard*.

Usage has decreed that the name Hansard has lived on in most countries that have adopted the parliamentary practices of Westminster. Yet, without Cobbett, *Hansard* would never be. But for a quirk of fate, parliamentarians in Canada and elsewhere would have their speeches reported in *Cobbett*. But then, William Cobbett, ploughboy, patriot and parliamentary reformer, does not need the indignity of remembrance in the phrase, "Mr Speaker, I rise to make a correction in *Cobbett*."

The Hansard Family Era

FROM 1812 until 1888 the Hansard family produced the *Parliamentary Debates*. Given the high standard of the reporting of parliamentary debates in Canada since 1880, it will surprise not a few to learn of the low quality of parliamentary reporting at Westminster during the almost eighty years while it was in the hands of the Hansard family. Until 1878, no bona fide reporters were employed by the Hansards; their reports were copied from the newspapers of the day, mainly *The Times*. In that year a subsidy was granted to the Hansard Company. Then, and only then, was the first *Hansard* reporter employed. Ten years later, however, complaints were still widespread, and in 1889 Henry, the son of T.C. Hansard, broke the family connection with the *Debates*.

There followed another unhappy period of contract reporting until, eventually, in 1909, Westminster established its own staff of official *Hansard* reporters. This ensured that the official and verbatim reporting of debates at Westminster reached the standard of excellence to which Canadian parliamentarians had been accustomed for the preceding twenty-nine years. In fact in 1907 a Select Committee recommended adoption of the Canadian system after a number of British MPs had visited Ottawa and Washington to learn how *Hansard* could best serve their Parliament:

> Indeed it was the result of a report made on the Ottawa *Hansard* by Lord Lee of Fareham that the reporting of parliamentary debates was made an official rather than a private undertaking in the United Kingdom.

Robert Rhodes James, a senior clerk at Westminster from 1955

23

to 1964, in his delightful book on the British House of Commons, deals with the matter in these words:

> Thus was the "Official Report" born in 1909 and "Hansard" killed. So deeply did the first editors of the new report despise the old version that the very word "Hansard" was not allowed to appear until 1943, when Mr Cornelius, the then Editor, daringly reintroduced it. But *Hansard* is what it has always been called, and what it will always be called.
>
> In 1909, when the Official Report undertook its tremendous task, there were ten reporters, soon increased to twelve. At one time in the last war the numbers fell to seven, but afterwards were raised to eighteen, of whom one was a woman. The department is paid by the House of Commons, and today consists of twenty-four persons, there being an Editor, an Assistant Editor, and two sub-editors, in addition to twenty reporters. The only proceedings of the House which the reporters do not record are those in Select and Private Bill Committees, which are handled by a private firm, Gurneys, which was first entrusted with this responsibility by the House in 1813.*

The reference to the "first editors of the new report" requires amplification. George Scott is writing about James Dods Shaw, the first Editor of Debates at Westminster.

> Shaw was a man of many parts, each of which he played with distinction and style. He had worked on the literary staffs of the *Liverpool Daily Post*, the *Leeds Mercury* and the *Manchester Guardian*. He wrote prolifically—of his holiday travels in Canada, Egypt, Siberia, Japan, China, Malaya and Ceylon; on antiquarian subjects as well as social and political ones. For many years he acted as the political correspondent of the Press Association. So respected was he that when in 1908 it was decided that there should be a verbatim report of all speeches in Parliament, and an official staff of reporters, Shaw was put in charge and became the first editor of *Hansard*. He was knighted in 1913. A man of considerable presence, he was always most meticulous in his dress. A colleague said of him that "he would as soon have been seen walking the streets in his night-shirt as he

*Robert Rhodes James, *An Introduction to the House of Commons* (London: Collins, 1961), p. 126.

would have been seen without his glittering top hat and spats; we often wondered if he slept in them."*

Having decided to adopt the Canadian system, it will be seen that Westminster adopted it well.

Richard Dring, current Editor of Debates at Westminster, reported in August 1978 that Dr John Hansard, last surviving member of the Hansard clan, has turned over all family papers connected with the enterprise to the University of Southampton.

A parliamentary milestone in the *Hansard* saga was reached in 1840 with passage of a statute that was a forerunner of the much touted and long heralded freedom of information legislation of the present day. The events leading up to it began in 1837 when a bookseller, John Joseph Stockdale, instituted a libel action against the Hansard family firm for publication of certain statements in their reports. The affair dragged on for more than two years. One of its highlights was the imprisonment of the two London sheriffs who served the originating writ.

Essentially what was involved was the privilege of Parliament to have its debates openly reported. The question was partially resolved in the 1840 enactment, which directed that proceedings launched against persons for the publication of papers printed by order of Parliament were to be stayed by the courts upon proof that their publication was carried out as a result of such parliamentary order. What has never yet been settled is the extent to which the privilege accorded to *Hansard* extends to newspapers that quote statements printed in *Hansard* reports.

Thus, while the Hansard firm was free to pirate newspapermen's reports—in effect operating a glorified press clipping agency—there remained the irony that newspapers quoting from *Hansard* continued to run the risk of being faced with litigation over the content of such quotations.

*George Scott, *Reporter Anonymous: The Story of the Press Association* (London: Hutchinson, 1968).

Parliamentary Reporting in Canada in the 1820s

WITHOUT the newspapers of the era, little would be known of the struggle to establish parliamentary democracy and "responsible government" in Upper Canada in the eighteen twenties. The weight of the establishment bore heavily on all aspects of pioneer life, and the early newspapers were largely instrumental in exposing this oppression. From 1819 to 1837 they published, or attempted to publish, full reports of the debates that took place in the Legislative Assembly or, as it was more popularly known, the Provincial Parliament, which met at York, later renamed Toronto.

One of the earliest references to the subject is found in Edward Allen Talbot's *Five Years' Residence in the Canadas*:

> Until 1820 the debates were not published; but since that period, two Irishmen, Carey and Collins, who are excellent stenographers, have been employed at an annual salary, to report, revise, correct, and publish the speeches. When they are thus skilfully got up and prepared, a man of a gentle, patient, and long-suffering disposition, if he were anxious for information on any of the subjects of debate, might perhaps *peruse them* without doing any great violence to his feelings: But to be doomed to listen to *the delivery of them* during a whole session, would be a much severer punishment, to a man of good taste and cultivated mind, than seven years' transportation to Van Dieman's Land.*

It is not surprising that Talbot was so scathing about the substance of the debates, while lauding the skill shown in the production of the printed record, because earlier in his work he gave the following description of the House of Assembly:

*Edward Allen Talbot, *Five Years' Residence in the Canadas*, Vol. I (London: Longman, Hurst, Rees, Orme, Brown and Greene, 1824), p. 411.

The House of Representatives, or Commons, is composed of forty members, who are a "motley crew" of all nations, trades, and professions, from the dusky blacksmith to the plodding lawyer . . . In Canada, instead of men of rank, fortune, and talents, you behold blacksmiths, tailors, tavern-keepers, and lawyers, debating the grave and important matters of State, in language graced with all the technicalities of their various professions, from which also they generally borrow apt and edifying illustrations.*

Talbot was no admirer of the common herd. To him, Robert Gourlay was "a political madman."† He was particularly down on blacksmiths. But the Canadian farrier has contributed much to the growth of Canada, politically and economically, and in the course of time a Canadian farrier's son was to become a much esteemed editor of *Hansard*.

The names John Carey and Francis Collins have been omitted from many works that purport to narrate the history of Canadian parliamentary reporting.†† It is to be hoped that the recognition which is their due, and which, to an almost perverse degree, has been denied them, will be given them now and in the future.

The story of Francis Collins appears at some length later in this narrative. That of Carey remains to be told fully in a future volume. However, an introduction to his life and achievements can be found in an article by Mary McLean.†††

The *Upper Canada Gazette* of 11 May 1820 carried the following notice: "The press and types from which the *Phoenix* issued, having come into the possession of J. Carey, the person who gave the debates of the House of Assembly during the last Session, it is his in-

*ibid., p. 401.

†Robert Fleming Gourlay was a Scot, born on 24 March 1778. He attended St Andrew's University, and advocated reform of the Poor Laws. In 1817 he became a land agent in Kingston, Canada, and a fearless critic of the Family Compact.

††See Elizabeth Nish, "Canadian Parliamentary Reporting" in *Debates of the Legislative Assembly of Upper Canada*, Vol. I (1841), reprinted by the Centre d'Etude du Quebec and the Centre de recherche en histoire économique du Canada français.

†††Mary McLean, "Early Parliamentary Reporting in Upper Canada," *The Canadian Historical Review*, Vol. XX (1939), 378-91.

tention to establish a newspaper in the town of York, to be entitled
the *Observer*."

Mary McLean writes:

> The *Observer*, established by John Carey in 1820, was to run for
> eleven years and yet today its worth must be determined by a mere
> handful of copies. Fortunately, for the purposes of a "Hansard" the
> debates, as reported by Carey, were faithfully copied by two Kings-
> ton papers of the time—the Kingston *Chronicle* and the *Upper Canada
> Herald*. Though at no time during the period was it financially
> possible for them to maintain their own reporters at York, their
> pages are an invaluable source of Carey's reports. The *Chronicle*,
> published by James Macfarlane, had a strong government bias and
> accepted the reports of the radical Carey only under protest. The
> *Herald*, published by Hugh Thomson, copied Carey's reports
> without comment and, editorially, had little to say on matters in the
> house.

Macfarlane's *Chronicle*, with its "strong government bias," was
to attack both Carey and Collins repeatedly in the years that followed. The struggle to protect freedom of parliamentary reporting
soon became a central part of the fight waged by the reformers
against the Family Compact. It was a see-saw affair: gains were
made in one year, only to be wiped out in the next.

In 1821 the House of Assembly passed the following resolution:
"That it is expedient that the debates of the House during the present session be reported, and that a stenographer or stenographers
be employed for that purpose and that the sum of £75 be appro-
priated to defray the expense thereof." Macfarlane did not like this
advance, and on 28 December wrote:

> The debates continued as usual from the York *Observer* are, we
> understand, jointly reported by the editor of that paper and the per-
> son who gave the debates of the last Session [i.e. Carey and Collins].
> With regard to the fidelity with which the work is executed we, of
> course, cannot judge from personal observation, but, though we
> believe that these gentlemen endeavour to be correct, we are also
> given to understand that their reports are frequently defective. Our
> readers must, however, rest satisfied with them, as there are no

stenographers in the Province capable of doing more equal justice to the orators who occupy the floor of Parliament.

No similar employment was offered for reporting the debates in the succeeding two sessions, but the reformers made another advance in 1825, when Francis Collins was employed by the House of Assembly. In the *Colonial Advocate* of 7 February 1825, William Lyon Mackenzie was to say of him: "From our knowledge of this reporter, we place implicit confidence in the general accuracy of his notes."

Macfarlane's *Chronicle* was still fulminating against Carey in March 1829 when, over the signature "Red-Hot Politician," it ran the following:

> There are four Newspapers established at the metropolis, and to their pages we must look for a report of the debates. Of the editors of these, one is a member of the House, and cannot be expected to give an accurate report of the debates. The Editor of the *Freeman*, who is a professed stenographer, is justly suffering from the punishment inflicted upon him for a gross libel on the administration of Justice ... The Editor of the *Loyalist* professes to give us a summary of the Debates; but, brief as this summary has been, it is now so far behindhand that it is uninteresting... The only one which remains to be noticed is the *Observer*, and its Editor appears to have exerted himself to the utmost of his abilities, to afford his readers the latest Parliamentary debates; but an impartial eye will soon discover the very great difference in the pains taken to report correctly the speeches of the *Observer's* friends and those of the party opposed to him in politics . . . .

Two years later, in 1831, the House of Assembly passed the following resolution:

> Resolved that Francis Collins, John Carey, and George Gurnett be Reporters to report the Debates and Votes of this House; that they shall report on successive days; that each reporter shall leave a fair copy of his report with the clerk, on the ensuing morning after each Debate, to which all proprietors of newspapers shall have access.

This appears to have been an equitable arrangement, but more lay beneath the surface than was exposed above it, and Messrs Carey and Collins were to decline their appointments.

On 22 November, the *Canadian Freeman*, published by Francis Collins, commented on the matter as follows:

> *Reporting.*—The House, this Session, are all for reporting, save Messrs Hagerman, Ketchum and Macnab—but George Gurnett is the only *bidable* tool they have got. We had the honour of an appointment, which we declined, as we disapproved of the conditions.

No wonder. As the publisher of the *Freeman*, Collins would have been subsidizing his journalistic rivals. There was an interesting sequel in the House, reported by the *Christian Guardian*, Egerton Ryerson's paper, in its issue of 7 December:

> A considerable discussion took place on the motion of Mr Samson to rescind the resolution of the house for employing reporters. Messrs Collins and Carey had declined reporting, not liking the conditions of the resolution for employing them, and the person employed by Mr Gurnett, it was argued, not being competent to the task, the resolution should be rescinded.
>
> *Mr Samson* observed that the reports were not correct . . . (Here he read an extract from a reported speech of the A.G. . . . which excited some laughter.) Such reports, Mr S. said, were calculated to mislead the public; and it was evident to every honourable member that the reporter was not competent, and the reports were garbled . . .
>
> *Mr Bidwell* was in favour of a reporter being paid by the house, as editors of newspapers could not bear the expense of employing them . . . He did not expect verbatim reports of the debates, but such a fair outline of them, that people might get a correct notion of what was said in the house . . .
>
> *Mr Samson* said that if the rule were rescinded, the house would come to an agreement to employ Mr Collins tomorrow. He had seen an advertisement in the *Courier* informing the public that a competent person had been employed to report for that paper during the present Session. He would read some of that person's reports. (Here Mr S. read some extracts which again excited considerable laughter.) The object of the present motion is only to get rid of the person who is now reporting, in order that a competent person may be employed.

Mr Mackenzie said that public opinion was in favour of reporting
. . . In every place where he had been the whole cry was "give us
reports" . . .
The house divided on the motion: Yeas 14, Nays 21, decided in
the negative by a majority of 7.

It was the newspapermen who supplied the early records of
debates in Upper Canada. The surviving newspaper files of the era
are the windows through which much of its history can be
surveyed. Mary McLean saw their true worth, and wound up her
study with an eloquent lament and plea:

> The great pity is that so little is being done to ensure the preserva-
> tion of these papers. We condemn our predecessors for their failure
> to hand on to us the complete files and yet surely our negligence in
> failing to preserve those that we have is infinitely greater than
> theirs. The librarians to whose assistance the writer is indebted are
> performing an important public service in maintaining their
> collections, but time and use will take their toll of files which cannot
> be replaced. At the present time it is to the original copies—the only
> ones—that the student must go. These papers must be photo-
> graphed—and that soon—if they are to fulfil their normal, and I
> believe vital, function as source-material for the history of Upper
> Canada.

The present writer wishes to pay tribute to the effectiveness of
her plea. The newspapers, as many of them as survive, have been
microfilmed and are readily available at the Public Archives and
through the Canadian Library Association to student and professional alike. Their worth is incalculable.

Louis Roy

TOURISTS visiting Upper Canada Village, a short distance from Morrisburg, on the banks of the St Lawrence, are intrigued to see a printing shop, fully operational, producing samples of the art of printing as it was practised in Canada in the early 1800s. Indeed, the newsprint used is especially manufactured according to the processes devised by the country's first papermakers.

Having left the printing shop, however, the casual visitor may miss one of the Village's rarest treasures, housed in another building. There, restored but not in daily functional order, although, considering its age, still in remarkably good preservation, stands a wooden printing press, a relic of the 1700s. It is the press on which was printed the first newspaper in Upper Canada, the press of Louis Roy, a name indelibly engraved in Canadian annals.

Although his press survives, the ultimate fate of Roy remains shrouded and uncertain, beyond the fact that his death took place in New York, shortly before 1800.* He was reputed to be the son of a French soldier who married and settled in Canada. He became an apprentice printer in the shop of the *Quebec Gazette*, the first newspaper established in Lower Canada in 1764. At a later stage in his career, he was also to establish yet another journal in Montreal, thus chalking up an amazing three firsts before vanishing from the scene.

Lieutenant-Governor John Graves Simcoe was the gentleman responsible for inducing Roy to leave Quebec and bring his types and press to Niagara, Ontario, then the capital of Upper Canada. Within a few months of his arrival, on 18 April 1793, Roy

---

*Christopher Porter, curator of technology at Upper Canada Village, gives the date of Roy's death as 24 September 1799, at age twenty-eight.

published the first issue of *The Upper Canada Gazette or American Oracle.*

It was an official journal, even though it was not explicitly stated as such. The Royal Arms appeared at the top of the first page, and its contents included a proclamation by Simcoe requiring all police officers and constables "to enforce the laws of England against blasphemy, profaneness, adultery, fornication, polygamy, incest, profanation of the Lord's Day, swearing and drunkenness." The Speech from the Throne to the British Parliament of 13 December 1792 was also reprinted, and "a transcript from a Philadelphia paper recording the debate in the House of Lords on the Aliens Bill."

Yet Roy, the first King's Printer in these parts, did not remain long at the post, but returned to Quebec in the following year and established the short-lived *Gazette de Montreal* on 17 August 1794. The paper he left behind in Upper Canada remained in sole occupation of the field until 1798.

The position of King's Printer was granted only to those who supported the administration, and woe betide any, such as Charles Fothergill, who questioned executive council decisions. Several who did were quickly replaced by sycophants, whose consciences remained unpricked at the sight of the many injustices perpetrated by the Family Compact.

Louis Roy can be seen as the forerunner of many Canadians of French extraction who found and still find themselves ill-at-ease when transplanted from their home environment. In Roy's case, however, not even a return to Montreal brought him solace, and after a little over a year he left his native province for the last time.

Louis Roy was a printer with itchy feet. He may, in truth, have been the original Canadian "peripatetic pressman on the prowl."

The King's Printers

THE early King's Printers were under severe pressure to conform to the strictures of the Lieutenant-Governor and the Family Compact. Their tenure in office was at the establishment's pleasure, and the slightest sign of democratic tendency in their reports was met with instant dismissal. The shortness of some of their appointments needs no further comment. They were: Louis Roy (14 April-10 July 1794); Gideon Tiffany (10 December 1794 -5 July 1797); Titus Greer Simons (20 September 1797-18 July 1801); William Waters (6 July 1798-13 August 1808); John Cameron (15 April 1807-25 November 1815); Edward McBride (9 December 1815-3 February 1816); Dr Robert C. Horne (2 January 1817-26 December 1821); Charles Fothergill (1 January 1822-12 January 1826); and Robert Stanton (19 January 1826-21 September 1844). Stanton, and for good reason, was the only one to last for any significant period of time. His immediate predecessor, Fothergill, was dismissed in 1826 for allowing the following sentence to appear in his newspaper: "I know some of the deep and latent causes why this fine country has so long languished in a state of comparative stupor and inactivity while our most enterprising neighbours are laughing us to scorn."

Contrast the treatment accorded the official printers in colonial times with developments in later years. True, the position remained one in the gift of the government of the day, but without the all-pervasive pressure to conform. Incumbents were generally left undisturbed, despite political changes in government ministries. Indeed, the only occasion in recent times that public notice was taken of the institution in any marked degree was with respect to the construction of the Government Printing Bureau in

Hull, Quebec. Donkeys on the payroll, or was it horses? Those opposed will please say nay. "Some hon. members: Neigh!"

Persecution and Prosecution of the Press

IF a succession of King's Printers laboured under political pressure, consider the difficulties faced by independent newspapermen who took an interest in the development of Upper Canada, and who, in varying degrees, attempted to educate the populace to the shortcomings of their rulers. Dismissal from office was a light penalty compared to fines and imprisonment on trumped-up charges of seditious libel. There are numerous examples. To give a flavour of the era just prior to the earliest serious attempts at parliamentary reporting, the prosecution in 1818 of Bartimus Ferguson, editor of the *Niagara Spectator*, may well be cited.

Ferguson and Robert Gourlay go together. Gourlay was the first real thorn in the side of the Family Compact. His story, however, is of little relevance to this chronicle, except that it shows the extent to which the authorities went in their efforts to curb the growth of an independent press. Their fears of Gourlay and of the success he was meeting were so great that they encouraged passage of an Act of Parliament of Upper Canada forbidding "assemblies, committees, or other bodies of persons, elected or otherwise constituted or appointed," to meet under the pretense of deliberating upon matters of public concern. Freedom of speech did not exist in colonial Canada. A group of three people could be hauled off to jail, for discussing politics!

Gourlay neatly summed up matters in the following lines, which were published in the *Niagara Spectator* on 3 December 1817:

> Gagg'd—Gagg'd, By Jingo!
> Dear, sweet Canada, thou
> art gagged at last.

CHAP. XI.

An Act to prevent CERTAIN MEETINGS within this Province.

[*Passed 27th November*, 1818.]

Preamble

WHEREAS, the election or appointment of Assemblies, purporting to represent the people, or any description of the people, under the pretence of deliberating upon matters of public concern, or of preparing or presenting Petitions, Complaints, Remonstrances, and Declarations, and other Addresses to the King, or to both or either Houses of Parliament, for alteration of matters established by Law, or redress of alledged grievances in Church or State, may be made use of to serve the ends of factious and seditious persons, to the violation of the Public Peace, and manifest encouragement of Riot, Tumult, and Disorder; It is hereby enacted by the King's Most Excellent Majesty, by and with the advice and consent of the Legislative Council and Assembly of the Province of Upper Canada, constituted and assembled by virtue of and under the authority of an Act passed in the Parliament of Great Britain, entitled, "An Act to repeal certain parts of an Act passed in the fourteenth year of His Majesty's Reign, entitled, 'An Act for making more effectual provision for the Government of the Province of Quebec, in North America, and to make further provision for the Government of the said Province,'" and by the authority of the same, That all such Assemblies, Committees, or other bodies of persons, elected or otherwise constituted or appointed, shall be held and taken to be unlawful assemblies, and that all persons giving or publishing notice of the election to be made of such persons or delegates, or attending, voting, or acting therein by any means, are guilty of a high misdemeanor; *Provided always*, That nothing in this Act contained shall impede the just exercise of the undoubted right of His Majesty's Subjects to petition the King or Parliament for redress of any public or private grievance.

Assemblies held for certain purposes, declared to be unlawful, and persons giving notice thereof or acting therein, held guilty of a high misdemeanor.

Not to interfere with the just exercise of the right of petitioning.

The "Gagging" Act of 1818.

A babe of mighty Wellington,
come o'er the sea
Has, with thy own foul fingers,
gagged thee.

The "babe of mighty Wellington" was the Lieutenant-Governor, Sir Peregrine Maitland, and the "foul fingers," the Family Compact. Maitland's predilection for gagging was to last throughout his entire administration. In 1824, after the foundation of the monument being erected to Isaac Brock on Queenston Heights had reached a height of fourteen feet, he ordered it dug out and the copy of the first issue of the *Colonial Advocate*, William Lyon Mackenzie's reform paper, removed from the cavity in which it had been deposited.

Gourlay's poesie brought an immediate reaction. Bartimus Ferguson, the editor, was imprisoned, although he was later released when the authorities deemed that the time was not ripe to continue with their prosecution.

In June of the following year the *Niagara Spectator* published a letter written by Gourlay who, by that time, was himself in jail on charges arising out of his crusade for reform. It was adjudged to be a libel, and, on 8 November 1818, Ferguson was "sentenced to pay a fine of £50, to suffer imprisonment for eighteen months, to stand for four hours a day during the first month in the public pillory, and to remain in prison until the fine was paid and security given." A plea against the severity of the sentence had some effect, and Ferguson was not forced to stand in the pillory. He served seven months of the sentence before being released. In 1832, in his fortieth year, he died at York.

Maitland succeeded in having Gourlay banished from Canada, thus stemming, for a few years, the initial movement in the tide of reform. A contemporaneous commentary on Maitland's action, by one who was himself opposed to reform, and who wrote of "the notorious Gourlay," puts the matter into proper focus.

In 1824 Edward Allen Talbot ended Volume I of *Five Years' Residence in the Canadas* with the following lines:

When I arrived in the country in 1818, he [Gourlay] was abiding his time at the Brockville Assizes for a libel on the Government. On hearing of his conduct in the Province, I was fully satisfied that he had plans in view of a more important nature than any he was willing to develope [*sic*] to the people of Canada. I recognized in him a link of that radical chain, with which in England the democrats were endeavouring at that time to fetter the honourable exertions of a ministry, whose wise and patriotic measures have conferred greater lustre on the British name, than ever had been before acquired in the field or in the senate. Whenever I had an opportunity, I represented Gourlay as the man whom, I thought, I had discovered him to be; but every person with whom I conversed on the subject, rejected my insinuations with disdain, and would hear nothing against this "great public benefactor." He was in truth, the idol of the people; and I do not doubt, that any imputation upon the character of our blessed Saviour would have been much more favourably received, by several of them, than the slightest objection to that political madman. The consequence of this universal infatuation was, that many of the most respectable persons in the province cultivated an intimate acquaintance with Gourlay; in which, I am convinced, they were not under the influence of any disloyal or disaffected views. When, therefore, he was banished from the country, in a very unconstitutional manner, his acquaintances, most of whom were officers in the militia and justices of the peace, were to a man deprived of their commissions, for the simple crime of having associated with Mr Gourlay. All these men, as it is generally allowed, were before this event as faithful subjects of his Majesty as any in the country, and had given ample proof of their loyalty in the recent combat with the United States. This, however, is a character, which, I venture to predict, they will not continue to maintain. Oppressive treatment will alienate even the affections of a child from its parent; and the arbitrary measures of a government professing to be free, especially when such measures are directed against innocent and unoffending individuals, must infallibly weaken the loyalty of a spirited and independent subject . . . Among other very unpopular acts of the present Lieutenant Governor, this is one which is the most revolting to the Canadians.*

*In 1842 the United Canada parliament declared Gourlay's banishment unconstitutional. Eighteen years later he was elected MP for Oxford County. He died in Edinburgh, Scotland, on 1 August 1863.

First Stirrings in Quebec

FOR generations it was a popularly accepted belief that only with the misnamed "Conquest" did the first stirrings of printing and journalism make an appearance within the boundaries of present-day Quebec City. Thanks to a little-known work, privately funded and little encouraged, it is now realised that a printing establishment did come into existence in the city, under the patronage of a far-sighted bishop, and was used to some effect during the famous siege in 1759. Be that as it may, it is incontrovertible that the province's first newspaper came into existence just a year later, with the founding of the *Quebec Gazette* by Brown and Gilmore, two Philadelphia printers. Its lineal descendent, the *Quebec Chronicle-Telegraph*, claims to be the longest published newspaper in North America, disputing the more generally acknowledged claim of the Hartford *Courant*.

In 1778 Fleury Mesplet brought the first Montreal newspaper into existence, grandiloquently styled *La Gazette du Commerce et Littéraire*, six years later to become the more simple *Montreal Gazette*. Monsieur Mesplet deserves more than a passing word in any work that deals with press freedom and parliamentary reporting in Canada.

He was a native of Lyons, France, and learned the printing trade in his own country. A restless man in his young days, a characteristic trait of printers throughout the world, Mesplet left France to find fame and fortune elsewhere. For a time he had a printing works in Covent Garden, London, but he then decided to sail to the United States. In Philadelphia he became swept up in all the fervour of the American revolution, and in 1786 was selected to accompany Benjamin Franklin to Montreal, which at that time was in American hands. A city of some 8,000 French-speaking inhabitants, Montreal was thought by Franklin to be fertile ground for republican propaganda. However, by the time Mesplet arrived there with his press and type, the Americans were on the point of retreating. The by now almost penniless Mesplet was thrown in jail by the first English troops to re-enter the city.

Fortunately, Fleury Mesplet had the only printing press in town; he was soon released and allowed to pursue his trade. Within two years he established his *La Gazette du Commerce et Littéraire*, but on 2 June 1779, one day short of its first birthday, publication was suspended. For the second time in his life, Fleury Mesplet was imprisoned. Depending on which version of events is read, he spent "three years in a filthy dungeon without trial," or was "interned," along with his editor, Valentin Jautard, by order of Governor Haldimand.

In 1782 Mesplet was "allowed to escape." This was a simple solution for the authorities. Having incarcerated him without trial, what easier way could they devise to end the affair than by allowing him to escape, and thus avoid the legal consequences of their actions? Three years later, in 1785, the much-penalized Mesplet reopened his padlocked newspaper, this time as the *Montreal Gazette / Le Gazette de Montreal*, a completely bilingual publication, which he continued to publish until his death in 1794. From France, to England, to America, to Canada, into jail and into the pages of history, Fleury Mesplet is a name not to be forgotten in the annals of men who suffered and fought for a free press to serve their fellow men.

Reporting of debates in the Quebec legislature was undertaken by the newspapers from the time of its establishment in 1792. Of these the more prominent were the *Quebec Mercury*, founded by Thomas Cary in 1805, and *Le Canadien*, established in 1806 by Pierre Bédard and François Blanchet. *Le Canadien*, a newspaper which in present times would be called "nationalist," was also padlocked, and was often forced to suspend publication. Both Blanchet and Bédard also saw the inside of jails in 1810, at the behest of Sir J. Craig, then

Governor-in-Chief of Canada, who took umbrage at their "unwelcome frankness" in the pages of *Le Canadien*.

The *Montreal Herald* was the next newspaper to be published in Quebec, in 1811. Later, in 1826, came *La Minerve*, one of whose editors, Joseph Ludger Duvernay, shared equal prominence with Dr Daniel Tracey, founder of the Montreal *Vindicator & Canadian Advertiser*, in as bizarre a story of parliamentary repression of the press as has ever been told in any country.

Another to suffer imprisonment for alleged libel against the government of the day was Jocelyn Waller, editor of *The Canadian Spectator*, also a Montreal paper. Waller had the audacity to use the word "nuisance" in connection with the Legislative Council! He was known as a gentle person, and was to die two years after his imprisonment.

A third reformer of note in this period was Dr Edmund Bailey O'Callaghan, an associate of Tracey in running the *Vindicator*.

Mesplet was a Frenchman. Yet, three of his most outstanding successors were Irishmen, Waller, Tracey and O'Callaghan.

Tracey of the *Vindicator*

DANIEL Tracey was a Tipperary man, born in the town of Roscrea in May 1795. His father, Michael, was a merchant. His mother, a Miss Mainfold, was the daughter of "a gentleman of family and fortune, residing in Erescourt, in the vicinity of Birr in King's County" (now renamed County Offaly).

The young schoolboy showed outstanding scholastic promise, and after four years study in Clonmel was qualified to enter Trinity College, Dublin as "a gentleman commoner." Prizes in classics and philosophy were to come his way, and a short sketch of his life, written as an obituary in 1832, indicates that his formal education continued:

> After graduating in the University, he entered the Royal College of Surgeons, in Stephen's Green, Dublin, where he devoted two years' close application to the study of physics and surgery. Leaving this institution with honorable diplomas and flattering attestations of his capabilities of shining in the profession which he intended to pursue, he commenced to practice in Dublin, and by the ingenuity and skill of his operations, as well as the affability of his conciliatory manners, soon acquired professional eminence. But the democratic spirit had taken too deep a root in his sensibilities to suffer him to remain in his beloved native land, while she was yet the victim of religious exclusion, and the martyr of English despotism.*

In 1825, his thirtieth year, Tracey, his brother John and sister Anne emigrated to Canada. He resumed the practice of medicine in Montreal. By that time the city had grown to a population of

---

*"The Irish Republican Shield" from *The Vindicator*, 26 February 1833.

43

30,000, a large increase from the 8,000 when Fleury Mesplet had first arrived there.

In early December 1828 Tracey launched the *Vindicator* newspaper. On the front page of the *Canadian Freeman* of 4 December 1828, the following advertisement appeared: "Prospectus of a new semi-weekly paper to be published in the city of Montreal under the title of 'The Irish Vindicator and Canada General Advertiser,' to be conducted by *Daniel Tracey and John Hogan*." In outlining the newspaper's aims, the prospectus made several declaratory statements, of which the following is representative:

> We have suffered too much in the land of our fathers to encourage in the land of our adoption any division among the people . . .
>
> To the local interests of Canada, her agricultural and mercantile concerns, the improvement of her cities and villages, her Schools, Colleges and other Institutions, we shall pay particular attention. There is one subject indeed on which, from its vast importance to mankind, we would wish to bestow every care: the Education of the People. This we will encourage by all means in our power, point out its benefits, and endeavour to convince those who think lightly on the subject, of its great effect, when properly bestowed, in reforming the morals and elevating the condition of mankind.

The *Vindicator*'s masthead motto, "Justice to all classes; monopolies and exclusive privileges to none," was a reaffirmation of the principles outlined in the prospectus. It was published on Tuesdays and Fridays and was a commercial success. Its political achievements can easily be measured by the severity of the steps taken by the Quebec Family Compact, the Legislative Council, in 1832 against the fearless Tracey, and against his editorial colleague on *La Minerve*, Ludger Duvernay, for alleged libellous criticism of the Council. At this stage the *Vindicator* had its own correspondent in Quebec City, who reported the debates of the Lower Canada Parliament on a regular basis.

In his article, "Dr Daniel Tracey, A Pioneer Worker for Responsible Government in Canada," Dr Emmet J. Mullally has written:

> On January 3rd of 1832 an editorial was printed in *The Vindicator* which, to newspaper readers of our time, appears very mild,

drawing attention to the way public affairs were administered by the Legislative Council. From the Journals of the Legislative Council for Lower Canada for 1831-1832 the following abstract was taken, reporting the sitting of that body for Thursday, January 12th, 1832. The members present were: The Honorable Chief-Justice Sewell, speaker; the Hon. Messrs Hale, Sir John Caldwell, Ryland, Cuthbert, Grant, Coffin, McKenzie, DeLery, Gugy, Felton, Bell, Stewart, Hatt, Moffat. The House resolved itself into a Committee of the Whole on a question of Privilege. The following resolution was drawn up and read on the following day, Friday, January 13th, 1832: "Resolved that the article headed 'Legislative Council' in the first column of the third page of the newspaper called *The Vindicator* of Tuesday evening the third instant Vol 4. No. 53, published in Montreal, contains a gross libel against this House and is a direct breach of its privileges." After an affidavit was read which had been drawn up in the name of a writing clerk of the Legislative Council to the effect that he had received copies of *The Vindicator* for two years, and had read the article complained of in the issue of January 3rd, which affidavit was sworn to before Chief-Justice Sewell on Friday, January 13th, it was moved in the Legislative Council, "that the Sergeant-at-arms do forthwith attach the body of Dr Daniel Tracey of the City of Montreal and bring him in safe custody to the Bar of this House, to answer for this offense and this shall be a sufficient warrant in that behalf."

A similar proceeding was adopted for the arrest of Ludger Duvernay, editor of *La Minerve*, Montreal, because he had printed an alleged libel in his newspaper.

When they appeared at the Bar of the Legislative Council on 17 January, Tracey and Duvernay, having acknowledged authorship of the articles in question, were "committed to prison in the common jail of the district of Quebec, for, and during the present session of the Provincial Parliament."

The two were in prison for thirty-five days. They were released when the Parliament prorogued, and on their return to Montreal were accorded a tumultuous reception. A medal was struck in their honour and, with much ceremony, a copy presented to each.

A little over a month later, in April 1832, a vacancy occurred in the representation for the West Ward of Montreal, a normally safe government seat. A Mr Stanley Bagg was put forward to represent the interests of the Family Compact, and Tracey decided to oppose him.

Duvernay, with the editorial reins of *La Minerve* back in his hands once more, actively promoted and encouraged Tracey's nomination. Urging his compatriots in Montreal to support Tracey in the election, Duvernay recalled that "the Irish had always supported the French in times of crises"—he might well also have stressed the converse—and praised Tracey's record of work for the community over the preceding seven years.

Today election campaigns in Canada are drawn-out affairs which at least have one saving grace, a fixed polling period, so that on the actual day of an election the result is known within a matter of hours. It was not so in Canada a hundred and fifty years ago. Polling lasted until it was evident that there were no more votes left to be cast. In the contest between Bagg and Tracey, polling lasted twenty-five days, with each day's tally being counted and published, so that from day to day everyone knew how the electorate was voting. The campaign began on 28 April and did not end until 22 May.

In present parlance, the governing party played "dirty pool" throughout the entire campaign. The returning officer was a lickspittle of the Compact, and did his utmost to manage events for their benefit, as the issue of *La Minerve* for 10 May makes plain:

> . . . during the last few days the returning officer has been obliged, on request of Dr Tracey and his friends, to announce that should no voter supporting Mr Bagg appear within an hour, he should be compelled to declare Tracey duly elected; a protest was served on the returning officer to the effect that he had changed the place of voting and he had failed to publish the customary proclamation when more than one hour had passed without anyone appearing to vote. Constables have been occupying the church grounds not far away from the polls . . .

The poll was situated on Place d'Armes Square. *La Minerve* added, "the political struggle drags slowly on."

Democracy, for which Duvernay and Tracey were fighting, was being throttled by officialdom. Every effort was made to thwart the will of the people. But what remains cause for wonder to this very

"Cholera Plague, Quebec City," painted c. 1832 by the Quebec artist Joseph Légaré (1795-1855). It hangs in the National Gallery of Canada.

day is that the violence, when it came, bubbled forth from the government side.

Both *La Minerve* and the *Vindicator* had reported that supporters of Tracey had been maltreated by a mob, but the real crunch did not come until the evening of Monday, 21 May. When it was over, three men lay dead on the streets of Montreal, and a score of others were injured.

On that day, Tracey had been leading Bagg by a mere three votes. A row broke out near the polling station in mid-afternoon, and the militia were called. Sixty soldiers were soon positioned at strategic spots.

When the poll closed at 5 o'clock, Tracey and a group of his supporters started for home, walking along St James Street. Some of Bagg's supporters started throwing stones at them. There was retaliation. The soldiers moved in. In the general mêlée, some of them were struck. Immediately the order to open fire was given. The soldiers began firing into the Tracey group. Three fell dead, a score were injured.

On the following day, the poll reopened at 8 a.m. One further vote was cast for Tracey, and when, after an hour, no other vote had been received for Bagg, the poll clerk, Monsieur Guy, in the absence of the returning officer, declared polling ended and Tracey elected, the final court being 691 to 687.

In an editorial on the atrocity, published shortly afterwards, Tracey wrote:

> It has come to a pass where we must know for certain whether the militia associated with a minority of egoists and partialists who have been hostile to the country and who have been courted as much possibly with a view to sinister motives as to others, shall in violation of the rights of citizens, become the murderers of the people, trample underfoot our privileges and blacken, by the low and unworthy act of shooting down innocent persons, the distinguished calling of the soldier.

Less than two months later, on 18 July, Daniel Tracey himself was dead, a victim of the cholera epidemic of that year. He was thirty-eight years old.

Mullaly sums up, with some feeling, in these words:

> The histories of Canada and England ascribe the gaining of Responsible Government in Canada, to England, following the report made by Lord Durham, who was sent to Canada with the powers of a Dictator and who landed in Quebec with a ship-load of retainers and baggage on May 28, 1838. In reality, Responsible Government in Canada was won through the sacrifice of the lives of many Canadian patriots by shooting and hanging; and the banishment of many others; by the destruction of much property, and by the self-sacrificing labors of the leaders; and among the pioneer leaders was the physician, editor and patriot, Dr Daniel Tracey.

Tracey was imprisoned for daring to exercise freedom of the press to express his views. Dr Edmund Bailey O'Callaghan, a fellow exile, friend and medical colleague, acted as assitant editor of the *Vindicator*. He managed the paper during Tracey's imprisonment, and succeeded him as its second and last editor. O'Callaghan had to flee the country to escape mob violence, while the destruction of the plant of the newspaper itself, on 6 November 1837, ushered in the rebellion of that year in Montreal. The inside pages of the last issue, dated 8 November, contain this vivid word picture of the incident:

> Darkness having by this time completely enveloped this organised band of lawless desperadoes, they proceeded to put into execution a plan previously arranged and determined upon, of attacking and destroying the printing establishment of the VINDICATOR newspaper . . .
>
> This paper has already made itself, and all concerned in it, obnoxious to the faction which has so long had its hoof on the necks of the people, and almost all means have been resorted to, to crush it. Tory priests have been found to preach against it from the pulpit; Legislative Councillors to harangue against it in the Legislative Council; disappointed politicians to burn it in the public streets, and their bullies to waylay and attack its unarmed editor, in the hope of putting him out of the way . . .
>
> On this gallant and honorable expedition against THE PRESS the tory mob proceeded, after committing the injuries above mentioned on the Honourable Mr PAPINEAU'S premises . . . . Fur-

nished with axes for the occasion, the mob at once proceeded to cut
down the IRON DOORS and window shutters by which our Printing Office is secured. They demolished afterwards the inner doors
and windows, and gutted, in a manner, all the basement story.
They next seized the cases of types and flung their contents bodily
into the street; broke into the editor's room, and destroyed all they
could lay hands on strewing the streets in front of the house with
books, papers &c. . . .

The above was composed "literally in the open air," in the street
next day. Thus did the mob, at the direction of their rulers, "crush
the only semi-weekly English newspaper, printed in this city, supporting Liberal principles."

The Origins of Parliamentary Reporting in the Maritimes

A S was the case in Upper and Lower Canada, in the Maritime provinces the attainment of freedom for parliamentary reporting in the legislatures was obstructed during the early nineteenth century. The struggle is recorded in more detail in Nova Scotia than in New Brunswick and Prince Edward Island.

Again it was newspapermen who were in the vanguard. The two names most prominent in Nova Scotia at the start of the reporting of the debates of the House of Assembly were Anthony Henry Holland and Edmund Ward. Holland, in partnership with his brother Philip, founded the *Acadian Recorder* in 1813, and Ward established the *Free Press* three years later in 1816. The *Recorder* espoused the cause of reform, while the *Free Press* was a Tory government organ. Both began reporting and publishing the debates of the House of Assembly in 1817. Their journalistic and political rivalry was such that bad feeling led to all-out editorial warfare, and the Irishman, Ward, brought the long-running feud to a head by suing Holland in 1821. It was not an edifying spectacle. The result was hardly conclusive, damages and costs of £9 and threepence being awarded to the plaintiff. Eventually Holland withdrew from the *Recorder*, which later came into the sole possession of his brother, Philip.

The "little Compact" in Nova Scotia, so nick-named after the Family Compact in Upper Canada, viewed the admission of reporters to the Assembly with disdain, and certain legislators were not slow to react whenever they felt the slightest affront. William Minns of the *Weekly Chronicle* was ordered to appear before the Bar of the House in 1823. One Edward Browne, in 1824, went so far as to request compensation for reporting the Assembly's debates "for the previous seven years." Not surprisingly, his request was shelved.

In 1824 George Young was instrumental in launching the *Novascotian*, which was to become the Maritimes' most famous newspaper. In the following year he felt obliged to seek permission formally from the Assembly to report its debates. Permission was granted, but two years later, when he sought to obtain a place below the public gallery, the better to take his notes, a motion to allow this was defeated by 22 votes to 8.

By 1826, the *Free Press* had tired of reporting the debates. Ward wrote in February of that year:

> There has been nothing done in the Assembly during the past week which it would be expedient to report . . . We shall however attend from time to time, and without fatiguing our readers or making reports which are only a second edition of the Journals, will give the debates upon subjects of moment, when they come under discussion.

Joseph Howe bought the *Novascotian* from Young late in 1827 for £1,050, payable over five years at £210 annually. There was no more powerful an advocate of parliamentary reporting than Howe. However, he well knew the strain involved, and, having exerted himself to the full, reporting a ten weeks' session, it was with relief that he greeted its ending in 1833 and turned his attention to other matters:

> Truly we have tarried long enough with the Senators—let us look abroad and see what other classes are achieving. We have beside us a mountain of Books, Magazines, Pamphlets and Newspapers, that have been accumulating for the last two months, unopened and unread. Like a Turk, in the dim twilight of his Harem, we scarcely know which to choose . . . .

By 1837 the reporters' right to record the debates was confirmed without reservation, and four years later the Assembly had advanced to the point where it engaged its own reporters and laid down rules for their conduct. These reporters had to supply the press with copies of their transcripts. However, the pendulum was to swing back, with official sanction once more being withheld for a number of years between 1842 and 1848. In the latter year, on the attainment of responsible government, a reporters' gallery was constructed, and two years later the Assembly once more chose to engage its own reporters.

There are many other names which should be mentioned in this all too brief account of a stirring period in the struggle to obtain freedom of the press and of parliamentary reporting in the Maritimes. The cost, as usual, was as severe in Nova Scotia as elsewhere throughout the Canadas. In 1829 William Milne of the Pictou *Colonial Patriot* was jailed because of his inability to pay debts, when his subscribers failed to pay their own accounts. "He was freed owing to the 'friendly interposition' of some faithful supporters," and on his release signified his intention to take payment for his paper in kind, in fact in "any kind of merchantable produce."*

Harsh though the treatment of the press was in Nova Scotia, there were no instances of the kind of physical harassment encountered in Newfoundland. There, the editor of the St John's *Ledger*, Henry Winton, had his ears cut off and was left unconscious by thugs who had been lying in wait for him after dark. His printer, Herman Lott, suffered the same fate. It is not known if the latter's wife rubbed salt into their wounds, but the authorities, unfriendly to the *Ledger*, made little attempt to apprehend the guilty parties. Further, a gentleman named Parsons, of the Newfoundland *Patriot*, was sentenced to three months' imprisonment in another incident, and ordered to remain there until he had paid a fine of £50.

Publication of certain types of "Letters to the Editor" in the nineteenth century led to many prosecutions for malicious libel. John Hooper of the *British Colonist* in Saint John, New Brunswick, was the victim of one such prosecution in 1831. He conducted his own defence, and after nineteen hours of deliberation, the jury could not agree on a verdict. In 1835, Joseph Howe was likewise prosecuted over publication of a letter in the *Novascotian*. This was

---

*J.S. Martell, "The Press of the Maritime Provinces in the 1830s," *The Canadian Historical Review*, Vol. XIX (1938) p. 27.

the famous Howe libel case that became a cornerstone in the establishment of freedom of the press in Canada. Howe, too, conducted his own defence, and the jury unanimously agreed on a verdict of not guilty. It was a remarkable triumph.

In New Brunswick all newspapers were published away from the seat of the legislature in Fredericton, and had to be content with the printed *Journals* for their reports. Finally some gentlemen in Saint John raised enough money to send a reporter to Fredericton for the express purpose of recording the legislative proceedings in 1831. This arrangement lasted for seven years, after which the legislature offered to pay half the costs of the service.

In Prince Edward Island all three or four newspapers were published in Charlottetown and had no difficulty reporting the debates.

To end this section of these chronicles, what better than a simple quotation from the renowned Howe, who wrote in 1830: "What is the use of the Press, if it is not to watch over—to reprove or to defend public men?"

Steps Along the Road

THE 1840 Act of Union that created one legislature for Upper and Lower Canada saw the struggle continue for the establishment of an official *Hansard*. John Byrom's petition of a century earlier, seeking permission "that a body may write shorthand in the cause of one's country," a petition he organized after being reprimanded for taking notes of the proceedings at Westminster, was still too radical a cry for many members of the new Union Assembly, which met for the first time in Kingston. However, in June 1840 it agreed to support Henry Fowler's *Mirror of Parliament* by subscribing for five hundred copies in English, with provision for a French translation to be made later. Yet within a month this support was withdrawn, no French translation was ever made, and no satisfactory resolution of the matter was reached until forty years later, some thirteen years after Confederation and the establishment of the House of Commons of Canada.

Nevertheless, many efforts were made throughout those forty years, and reference must be made to a few hardy souls who, convinced of the worth to the country of a written record, would not let the issue die. In 1849 Ludger Duvernay, former fellow inmate with Dr Daniel Tracey of the Quebec common jail, petitioned for assistance to report and publish the Assembly's proceedings, but without success.

Newspapers continued to report selected speeches, many slanted according to the political leanings of the respective newspaper editors, some of whom were themselves members of the Assembly or Legislative Council. In 1850 an incident occurred which led to a boycott of the Assembly by the Press Gallery. The story is well told by Jesse Edgar Middleton:

The Journal of the Legislative Assembly for July 19th, 1850, says: "Mr Christie of Gaspé rose in his place and informed the House that yesterday evening while he was in conversation, and as he thought, in an undertone, from within the Bar of the House, with a person outside the Bar, he was addressed in a rude and offensive manner by a person in the reporters' box, whom he immediately after ascertained to be a Mr Ure, reporter to one of the papers published in this City [Toronto], who desired the informant to cease his talking, which, he said, prevented him from hearing what was going on in the House. Mr Christie followed the reporter outside and demanded an apology which Mr Ure declined to make. He said: 'You were talking and making a noise by setting two other persons near you at laughter, so that I could not do my duty . . . ' "*

Any *Hansard* or committee reporter can readily sympathize with Ure's plight. Casual conversation across the aisle of the House, or in committee, can be distracting to the individual trying to report a none-too-audible speech.

The upshot was that Ure was summoned to the Bar of the House and reprimanded by the Speaker:

One sentence of the reprimand follows: "You are totally mistaken as to your position. You are no part of this House and have no pretended position to maintain or duty to perform which can interfere with the privileges of Members or give you any right over them."

Immediately after this pronouncement, all the reporters in the Press Gallery downed pencils and walked out. For more than two weeks they boycotted the Assembly, members' speeches went unreported in the newspapers, and the result was telling to both parties.

On 31 July the members of the Press Gallery drafted a petition to the Assembly, from which the following paragraph is extracted:

That inasmuch as the whole people of the province cannot personally be present at such proceedings of your honourable House, it

---

*J.E. Middleton, *The Municipality of Toronto—A History*, Vol. I (Toronto: The Dominion Publishing Company, 1923), pp. 420-21.

is the opinion of the undersigned that the reporters of the Press—in
addition to their right to be admitted as a portion of the public—
ought also to be provided with suitable accommodation, so as to be
enabled to make known the proceedings of your honourable House;
and ought furthermore to be protected from such annoyance as may
prevent or impede the publication of your proceedings . . . .
And your petitioners as in duty bound will ever pray,—

Middleton gives a photographic facsimile of the signatures to
this petition: H.N. Scobie, *British Colonist*; George Brown, Toronto
Globe; S. Thompson, *Toronto Patriot*; Charles Lindsey, *Examiner*;
John Popham and Edward Ward, reporters, *Patriot*; M. Cooke and
J. Gordon Brown, reporters, *Globe*; Thomas de Walden, reporter,
British Colonist; Edward Goff Penny, *Montreal Herald*; G.P. Ure,
reporter, *Globe*; C. Donlevy, *Mirror*; and W. Kingston & Co., *North
American*.

With the ending of the session the matter was dropped. At the
start of the following session, reporters and members resumed their
respective places.

The issue of establishing a Canadian *Hansard* dragged on, and
on, and on. Session after session—in 1854, 1855 and 1857—the
question arose. French-speaking members generally favoured the
project. By now, certain English-language newspapers had a
vested interest in opposing an official report. In 1858 George
Brown of the Toronto *Globe* advocated the establishment of a scrapbook *Hansard*, with a librarian selecting and pasting into it each
morning from the various newspapers "the best report of each
speech." John A. Macdonald, who was then in his forty-third year
—prime ministership and knighthood still lay well in the future—
took the opposite tack, hoping for the establishment of an official
report, something which would save the public at large "the necessity of reading the *Colonist* and *Leader* as well as the *Globe*, in order to
see fully both sides of the question under debate."* In 1858
Georges Étienne Cartier also supported the establishment of a
Hansard.

The legislators reached agreement about the principal political

*Parliamentary Debates, 5 March 1858.

development of the 1860s, at least. Realizing the importance of
Confederation to the future of the country, Parliament decided to
have the debates on that subject fully reported. This was done on a
contract basis, however, and the unexpectedly high cost of the service provided fresh ammunition to those who, for the next thirteen
years, were to oppose the appearance of a permanent, official
Hansard in Canada. In that period there appeared the Scrapbook
Hansard, along the lines suggested by George Brown, and various
versions of a contract *Hansard,* of which the Cotton *Hansard* is the
most well-known. This "printed compilation of newspaper reports
for the sessions 1870, 1871 and 1872" was named after John Cotton
of the *Ottawa Times.*

To return briefly to the Confederation debates: George C.
Holland, who was one of the reporters of those historic speeches, in
later years, in partnership with his brother Andrew, secured the
contract to report the debates of the Senate of Canada. And in case
the latter august body may be viewed by some as staid and
hidebound in tradition, it must be recorded that the brothers
Holland "made regular use of the typewriter in the Senate some
years before this now indispensable machine became a part of the
equipment of the House of Commons."*

Frank Yeigh preserves the names of two other shorthand reporters of the Confederation debates:

> Mr William Buckingham, the joint author of the recently published
> 'Life of Alexander Mackenzie,' came to Canada in the fever of the
> agitation, in 1857, for the principle of representation by population,
> and immediately joined the staff of the *Globe* as shorthand writer . . .
> Mr Edwards, who afterwards removed to Washington and there
> died, was the regular hand with Mr Buckingham at that time on the
> *Globe.* They were afterwards associated with each other in Quebec
> in reporting officially the Confederation debates, regarded at the
> time as a great feat in the "winged art."†

---

*The quotation is from an address given in April 1932 by A.C. Campbell, former Editor
of Debates in the House of Commons.

†Frank Yeigh, *Ontario's Parliament Buildings* (Toronto: Williamson Book Company,
1893). See the chapter entitled "The Reporters' Gallery".

The sixty years from the time of John Carey and Francis Collins in the 1820s until the establishment of an official *Hansard* staff in the Canadian House of Commons were an exciting period of growth in the body politic. Much remains to be drawn in detail. The compilation of parliamentary debates prior to 1840 is a monumental task that must be undertaken before the full legislative history of Canada is placed before present and future generations. The staff of Canada's *Hansard* has been honoured to have been entrusted with that portion of the work extending over the past one hundred years.

The *Mirror of Parliament*

I N 1860 when the United Parliament was sitting in Quebec City, another attempt was made to report the debates. The gentleman responsible, Samuel Thompson, wrote an autobiography that sheds light not only on parliamentary affairs but also on life in Canada in the middle of the last century. On the title page of his book, *Reminiscences of a Canadian Pioneer*, he described himself as *Formerly Editor of the "Toronto Daily Colonist," the "Parliamentary Hansard," &c., &c.*

The *Parliamentary Hansard* is Thompson's *Mirror of Parliament*, which he published in Quebec City in 1860, and which was one of the forerunners of Canada's official *Hansard*, begun in Ottawa twenty years later. Thompson occupies a unique position in the history of the recording of Canadian parliamentary debate, suffering a greater monetary loss than any of his predecessors.

Although he was born within the sound of Bow Bells, Thompson claimed Scottish ancestry. His father died in the year he was born, 1810, but Thompson has left a description of him:

> He was a member of the London trained-bands, and served during the Gordon riots, described by Dickens in "Barnaby Rudge." He personally rescued a family of Roman Catholics from the rioters, secreted them in his house on Holborn Hill, and aided them to escape to Jamaica, whence they sent us many valuable presents of mahogany furniture, which must be still in the possession of some of my nephews or nieces in England.*

As a boy of thirteen, Thompson was apprenticed as a printer.

---

*Samuel Thompson, *Reminiscences of a Canadian Pioneer* (Toronto: Hunter, Rose & Company, 1884), p. 11.

For seven long years was I kept at press and case, working eleven hours a day usually, sometimes sixteen, and occasionally all night, for which latter indulgence I got half a crown for the night's work, but no other payment or present from year's end to year's end. The factory laws had not then been thought of, and the condition of apprentices in England was much the same as that of convicts condemned to hard labour, except for a couple of hours' freedom, and too often of vicious license, in the evenings.*

As a printer, he came in contact with many of the printing establishment's customers and absorbed much of their thinking and philosophy. When the young Thompson was expanding his horizons, Cobbett's days were drawing to a close, and, although nowhere in his reminiscences does Thompson mention Cobbett by name, he could not fail to have been influenced by his work. He tells us he became "a zealous Reformer," who heartily applauded his elder brother who refused to pay taxes when the first Reform Bill was rejected by the House of Lords.

Samuel Thompson forsook the printing trade in favour of the lumbering business, and at the age of twenty-three sailed for Canada and a new life. Among his first acquaintances in Toronto were the brothers Todd: Alfred, who was to become a committee clerk in the Canadian House of Commons, and his more famous brother, Dr Alpheus Todd, parliamentary procedural authority and parliamentary librarian. Thompson also met William Lyon Mackenzie, "at his printing office on Hospital Street," and was not impressed. Indeed, he tells two stories discrediting the future revolutionary.

With the passage of time, Thompson fell prey once more to the lure of printer's ink, becoming editor of the *Herald* newspaper and claiming independence from the patronage of Lord Sydenham, of whom he was to write in later years: "To connect in any way with his name the credit of bestowing upon the united provinces 'Responsible Government' upon the British model, is a gross absurdity."†

Thompson has a story to tell in this connection that will gladden

*ibid., p. 13.

†ibid., p. 114.

the hearts of old newspapermen who are familiar with an almost defunct custom, the issuance at Christmas or New Year's of a card presented by delivery boys to their customers:

> We used to issue on New Year's Day a sheet of doggerel verses, styled, "The News Boy's Address to his Patrons," which gave me an opportunity, of which I did not fail to avail myself, of telling His Excellency some wholesome truths in not very complimentary phrase. It is but justice to him to say, that he enjoyed the fun, such as it was, as much as anybody, and sent a servant in livery to our office, for extra copies to be placed on his drawing-room tables for the amusement of New Year's callers, to whom he read them himself. I am sorry that I cannot now treat my readers to extracts from these sheets, which may some centuries hence be unearthed by future Canadian antiquaries, as rare and priceless historical documents.*

Reminiscences of a Canadian Pioneer contains material much of which is the result of personal observation and judgment, but perhaps nowhere does the reformer Thompson show through more than in the following passage, in which he refers to the 1837 Rebellion:

> Lower Canada was never consulted as to her own destiny. Because a fraction of her people chose to strike for independence, peaceable French Canadians were treated bodily as a conquered race, with the undisguised object of swamping their nationality and language, and over-riding their feelings and wishes. It is said that the result has justified the means. But what casuistry is this? What sort of friend to Responsible Government must he be, who employs force to back his argument? To inculcate the voluntary principle at the point of the bayonet, is a peculiarly Hibernian process, to say the least.†

All this came from the pen of a man who believed himself to be throughout his life, "an Englishman of the English, a loyal subject of the Queen, and a firm believer in the high destinies of the Pan-Anglican Empire of the future."

*ibid., p. 161.

†ibid., p. 164.

Thompson's newspaper career in Toronto was a varied one, spanning the *Herald, Daily Colonist,* and *News of the Week.* During this period he saw the Dominion legislature move from Toronto, to Montreal, to Quebec, in a parliamentary merry-go-round. In 1859 Thompson removed to Quebec City, having secured the contract for parliamentary printing. There, for the session of 1860, he published his *Thompson's Mirror of Parliament,* and a newspaper besides, the *Advertiser.* And there, too, he found himself *in terra incognita.*

Unaware of the fact that previous contractors had included in their prices a portion for certain functionaries of the legislature, Thompson's bill was lower than his predecessors'. He justified this by claiming that his knowledge of printing placed him in a position of advantage over most of his competitors. In all, his expenditure on type, equipment and printing presses came to $45,000. Alas for Thompson, for his *Mirror of Parliament,* and for his adopted country, the venture went awry from the very start:

> When the Session had commenced, and I had with great outlay and exertion got everything into working order, I was refused copies of papers from certain sub-officers of the Legislature, until I had agreed upon the percentage expected upon my contract rates. My reply, through my clerk, was that I had contracted at low rates, and could not afford gratuities such as were claimed, and that if I could, I would not. The consequence was a deadlock, and it was not until I brought the matter to the attention of the Speaker, Sir Henry Smith, that I was enabled to get on with the work.*

Smith was a strong Speaker. But Thompson was to face difficulty from another quarter. The joint committee on printing, chaired by a Mr Simpson representing Bowmanville, cut the contracted amount of printing by one third.

> I struggled on through the session amid a hurricane of calumny and malicious opposition. The Queen's Printers, the former French contractor, and, above all, the principal defeated competitor in Toronto, joined their forces to destroy my credit, to entice away my

*ibid., p. 298.

workmen, to disseminate but too successfully the falsehood, that my
contract was taken at unprofitable rates, until I was fairly driven to
my wits' end, and ultimately forced into actual insolvency.*

The culmination of the affair was that Thompson was obliged to
give up the *Advertiser*, after running afoul of Georges Étienne
Cartier, friend of John A. Macdonald and one of the principal
architects of Confederation. For giving publicity to the complaint
of some dockworkers that they had been dismissed from their employment because they were Protestants (as Thompson put it, "I
think Orange") and for denigrating the merit of French institutions vis-à-vis those of Britain, "from that moment, it appears, I
was considered an enemy of French Canadians and a hater of
Roman Catholics . . . I was informed that Hon. Mr Cartier desired
that I should discontinue the *Advertiser* . . . He vouchsafed no argument; said curtly that his friends were annoyed; and that I had
better give up the paper."†
The end came shortly afterwards.

I knew that years before, the printing office of a friend of my own—
since high in the public service—had been burnt in Quebec under
similar circumstances. I could not expose my partners to absolute
ruin by provoking a similar fate. The Protestants of the city were
quite willing to make my cause a religious and national feud, and
told me so. There was no knowing where the consequences might
end. For myself, I had really no interest in the dispute; no prejudices
to gratify; no love of fighting for its own sake, although I had
willingly borne arms for my Queen; so I gave up the dispute; sold
out my interest in the printing contract to my partners for a small
sum, which I handed to the rightful owner of the materials, and left
Quebec with little more than means enough to pay my way to
Toronto.††

*ibid., p. 301.

†ibid., p. 314.

††ibid., p. 316. The partners were Robert Hunter, George M. Rose, John Moore and
François Lemieux.

Thus ended another chapter in the struggle to establish independent parliamentary reporting in Canada. Samuel Thompson's role in that struggle must not be allowed to be forgotten.

Francis Collins: "Cast a Cold Eye . . . "

FRANCIS Collins died of cholera, a hideous disease, at eight o'clock on Friday, 29 August 1834. His body was buried in old St Paul's cemetery on Power Street in Toronto. Where it is now, no one knows. There is no marker; there were no records. The cemetery itself is no longer there. Most of its inmates were removed to St Michael's, high above the bay of Toronto, at various stages in the late 1800s. St Michael's is now closed. One of Collins's daughters, Mrs Margaret Hayes, wife of Finbar Hayes, a former chief translator in the House of Commons, is buried there. So is his son, Francis Phelim O'Neill Collins. But the resting place of the man's own remains is unknown.

Collins prophetically left us a starkly vivid picture of his own burial. Describing the 1832 cholera plague, he wrote:

> During the existence of the late malady, bodies were interred at twilight, sometimes by aid of lanterns, sometimes clandestinely in the dark . . . we would like to see an Act of Parliament prohibiting graveyards altogether in populous parts of towns and villages.

Collins's funeral conveyance was not a hearse, but a loathsome cholera car. There was little time for mourning. It was a time of plague and the bodies of the dead had to be put underground as quickly as possible. Whether there were coffins for all the corpses is unknown. The gravediggers could scarcely keep up with their work.

Yet the spirit of Francis Collins is not dead. That spirit lives on, and in the most unlikely of places, in the Parliament of Canada in Ottawa, a place that was wilderness when Collins first trod Canadian soil.

There was no city of Ottawa then—no Bytown. The site of the present seat of the government of the Dominion of Canada was a dense, unbroken forest, an uncultivated wild, a pathless wilderness, where the bear and the wolf roamed uncontrolled, and the red deer gambolled in its deep, dark glades and sylvan retreats.*

Each time a *Hansard* reporter walks into the Chamber of the House of Commons to take down in shorthand or by stenotype the speeches of Canada's parliamentarians, thus transcribing the daily legislative history of the country, he or she embodies the symbolic spirit of Collins, the first such professional reporter, who occupies now, as in his own lifetime, pride of place in the annals chronicling Canada's parliamentary reporting.

The story of Francis Collins goes far beyond the confines of a narrowly specialised profession. It embraces fundamental principles of free speech and liberty of the press, sheds light on an era crucial to the development of democratic institutions, and provides a chapter of personal courage in the face of adversity.

Collins was born in the town of Newry, County Down, Ireland.† The exact date is untraceable. It has generally been ascribed to 1801, but may have been a few years earlier. His father was a printer who could afford to pay for his children's education. This was at a time when the hedge schoolmasters of Ireland were moving back into the towns, when the Penal Laws proscribing the vast majority of the population from receiving any instruction of any kind were slowly, ever so slowly, being relaxed. The first Christian Brothers' school to be established in Newry in 1805 has no attendance records for Francis or his older brother, John.

From his unknown tutor or tutors Collins received, to use a favourite descriptive adjective of his own, a "tolerable" education. He spent six years at Latin, and this experience led him to counsel against its being taught in the lower public schools that were later established in Canada. A pragmatist, he found little of value in it as

---

*Alexander Fraser, *The Last Laird of MacNab* (Toronto: Imrie, Graham & Company, 1889).

†Governor-General Guy Carleton, "Honest" John Lawless, Francis Collins and, through Lawless, William Cobbett, all had connections with Newry. All play a part in the story of *Hansard*.

training for a life to be spent in commerce or other material pursuits.

For him, an accomplishment much more worthily achieved than mastery of Virgil and Horace was the ability to set type. Growing up in a printing milieu, his greatest possible ambition was to compose his name with his own hand, painstakingly letter by letter, and to print it by himself, unaided by older brother, father or uncle. At the time it was self-gratification, but as the years went by, first in Ireland and later in Canada, the printed name of Francis Collins came to mean much more than self-fulfilment. To some it became like a red rag to a bull, to others it signified a radical, a reformer, one who spoke for the common man.

Four years ago Francis Collins's name could be found in his native land only in directories. It was known that there had been a Francis Collins, that he had been a Newry printer, and that he had published a newspaper. The stress placed on his being a Newry printer is deliberate. This was a town where, as early as 1756, two weekly newspapers were being published. Yet not one single copy of Collins's newspaper first published on 17 March 1814 was to be found in the mid-1970s in any library or archives in Ireland or the United Kingdom. Only a satirical "Letter to the Editor," printed in pamphlet form by Thomas Andrew in Derry city in 1815, remained as tangible evidence that there had actually been a paper. And it should be added that Collins by then had removed his base of operations to Belfast.

Yet, *mirabile dictu*, in 1977 was discovered, packed in wadding in the back of an old armchair, an almost unbelievably well-preserved copy of *The Ulster Recorder*, a four-page newspaper, dated Belfast, Friday, 8 September 1815, carrying the following imprimatur:

BELFAST
Printed and Published by
FRANCIS COLLINS, at the OFFICE
of *The Ulster Recorder*, 17,
Corn-market, every
Tuesday & Friday—
TERMS, £2 5s. 6d. per
annum, paid in advance.

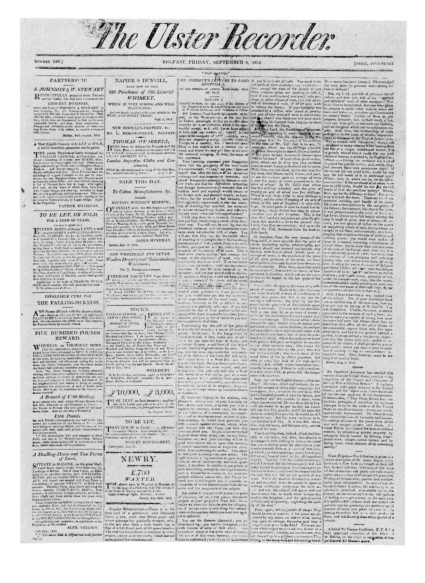

The front page of Collins's "most respectable opposition newspaper in Ireland," with a reprint of William Cobbett's correspondence.

As far as can be determined, No. 136 is the only extant issue.

The Ulster Recorder, like its successor, the *Canadian Freeman*, was a remarkably cleanly printed sheet. It was originally published at Newry. Its price was fivepence, of which twopence was paid in stamp duty. In 1815 a dozen eggs cost fivepence in Belfast.

Of singular interest is the masthead motto "Fiat Justitia," re-adopted by Collins in later years in Canada. Of paramount interest is the appearance on page one of two-and-a-half columns of correspondence written by the redoubtable William Cobbett in reply to a speech delivered by Lord Sheffield on the subject of the wool and grain trades. Collins's early acquaintanceship with Cobbett's work is thus firmly established. In his letter, Cobbett makes reference to the Corn Bill adopted in England "with regular troops drawn up round the House of Commons."

The satirical "Letter to the Editor of the Ulster Recorder," mentioned above, shows how effective was the *Recorder*'s impact on the thin-skinned opponents of parliamentary reform. The following extract provides further illustration of the newspaper's influence:

> When you are reporting Parliamentary debates, you can mutilate and disfigure some, dress and ornament others, as will best suit your purpose. You will also do the same with the speeches of other meetings. As you have already shewn your abilities in that line, we will expect your continuance . . .
>
> However, let me beg of you to be circumspect as to what you insert in your columns, and always keep the fear of the Attorney General before your eyes. It was owing to the obscurity and insignificance of the *Belfast Magazine* that it escaped the legal criticism of Mr Saurin, and though it courted prosecution it met with contempt, and sunk into oblivion.

The Ulster Recorder was suppressed in 1815, allegedly for non-payment of stamp duties. Francis Collins placed the blame for this action squarely on Castlereagh's shoulders. A few years later John Lawless, the newspaper's editor, was to claim that the *Recorder*, before its demise, had a circulation of 2,500 copies weekly.

The Governance of Upper Canada

A brief description of the Province of Upper Canada and of the town of York, where Francis Collins landed in 1818, is essential to an understanding of his subsequent career as parliamentary reporter and newspaperman. John Graves Simcoe was the first Lieutenant-Governor sent out from England to rule the colony. He was a man of military background, of undoubted personal courage, and of a set bent of mind. He envisioned the creation of a society based on class and hereditary privilege, thus setting in motion a train of events leading to the placement of power in the hands of a few families, the now notorious Family Compact, a name of derision derived from the interlocking treaties and marriage relationships of the Bourbons, of whose dynasty it is said that they never learned anything, and never forgot anything. The colonists were to have a parliament, with open elections, but Simcoe reserved all real power, the power of the purse and of appointment, to himself and an executive council, nominated by himself.

The first seat of government was at Newark, but in 1793 Simcoe determined on moving the whole apparatus of government and legislature to a new capital located on the Bay of Toronto. There had been French settlers and traders connected with Toronto since the mid-1600s, but when Simcoe decided that the bay would make a good naval base for the defence of Lake Ontario, he also decided to change the Indian name, Toronto, to York. Ironically, it had already been changed to Dublin on maps prepared by the Surveyor-General's office, the present Scarborough being named Glasgow, while Whitby was designated as Norwich. Simcoe would have none of that, and York it became, in honour of the famous Duke of

71

York, "who had ten thousand men . . . . " The city reverted to its
original name in 1834.

The Family Compact was made up of a few families who did
their utmost to protect their privileges and preferred places against
the inexorable pressure for reform. The Joneses, the Sherwoods,
the Macaulays, the Hagermans, the Robinsons and others enjoyed
a term of twenty years almost without opposition. The one big
flare-up stimulated by Robert Gourlay ended with his banishment
from the colony in 1819, a year after Collins's arrival. At that time
the administration was carried on by Sir Peregrine Maitland.
Lieutenant-Governor Maitland "had the power of force, Gourlay
only the power of speech. Speech had to give way to force in the
end."* Yet Maitland has long since given way, and Gourlay's stat-
ure has increased as the long living symbol of opposition to repression.

While speech dies, the written word remains. The new reformers, the Baldwins, Rolph, the Bidwells, whose speeches were
reported in shorthand by Collins, in conjunction with William
Lyon Mackenzie and John Carey, relied on the printed word to
transmit their message of reform to the general public, to spur its
members to exercise the franchise responsibly and to agitate for the
good and common goal of responsible government. Eventually
they were to succeed, but not without cost.

Maitland lasted ten years as Lieutenant-Governor. His successor, Sir John Colborne (1778-1863), another in the long line of
military men to be entrusted with the governance of Upper
Canada, took office in 1828. He was immediately faced with the
case of Francis Collins, by then the most prominent lodger in His
Majesty's local jail. Colborne refused to exercise his perogative to
extend clemency to Collins, although petitioned to do so by the
legislature and by numerous public meetings throughout the
colony. However, he was an improvement on Maitland and
encouraged many developments in the colony.

Simcoe's legacy, Maitland's obdurance, and Colborne's

*D.B. Read, *The Lieutenant-Governors of Upper Canada and Ontario 1792-1899* (Toronto:
William Briggs, 1900), p. 122.

washing of hands were three of the obstacles to reform in Upper Canada in the early part of the last century. Eventually they were to provoke Mackenzie to an abortive rebellion, and reform did come. But by then Mackenzie was a refugee in the United States, Carey was a candidate for retirement, "a portly figure who could be mistaken for a man of the cloth," and Francis Collins was lying, for a time undisturbed, in the graveyard known as St Paul's cemetery, on Power Street, Toronto.

Collins the Man

IN physical appearance, Collins was the archetypical Celt. According to Scadding, he was "a man of pronounced Celtic features, roughish in outline, and plentifully garnished with hair of a sandy or reddish hue."* His eyes were blue, he wore a beard and was of average height. That he had no deformity of body can safely be assumed. With the type of enemies he made, political and journalistic, any physical defect would have been mercilessly caricatured. Francis Collins had a sense of humour. He laughed at the foibles of others, and just as readily at his own.

In spirit he was adventuresome, curious and determined. He was not out of his teens when he disembarked at New York, some time before making the journey to Upper Canada, but had already at least one exciting career under his belt, publisher of a crusading reform newspaper, terminated by official sanction. He found employment almost as soon as he arrived in York, with Dr Robert C. Horne, then the King's Printer, and made arrangements to petition for the normal 100 acres of land available to all who could meet the necessary conditions. He did likewise for his brother John, who was to follow him in the fall of 1819, and for a third Newry man, Michael Daly.

Six years after reaching York, Collins had prospered to the extent that he could afford to travel back to Ireland to marry his childhood sweetheart, Ann Moore, and return with her to Canada. She was the daughter of a prominent family, an aunt of Lord Russell of Killowen (later to become Chief Justice of England), and of the celebrated Rev. Matthew Russell, S.J. A year later, in

*Henry Scadding, *Toronto of Old: Collections and Recollections* (Toronto: Adam, Stevenson & Company, 1873), p. 191.

1825, their first child, Mary, was born. In the first week of June in the same year the *Canadian Freeman* was born, "Printed and Published by F. Collins, New-street, one door north of Market-square, at £1 per annum, payable in advance."

Nine years later, Francis Collins, his wife Ann and their daughter Mary perished, all within the space of a week, victims of the cholera epidemic of 1834.

That he was a curious man can be deduced from his own writings, and from the words of Pliny the Elder that he chose to adorn the *Freeman*'s masthead, *Est natura hominum novitatis avida*, "Man is by nature fond of novelty." Curiosity in a newspaperman is a natural quality, and Collins had ample scope in which to observe the burgeoning life of his adopted country, happily situated as he was at the seat of government. From his curiosity came knowledge of men and events, knowledge that he shared with his fellowmen, and from that knowledge came the determination to follow once again the path of reform, even if it were to lead to trials and tribulations far in excess of any he had suffered in his native land. And so it happened that fate itself determined the replacement of his motto with one already blooded in battle and much more in keeping with the man and his background, *Fiat justitia, ruat coelum*, "Let Justice be done tho' the Heavens fall!" Indeed, it is recorded that, to the Celts of Vercingetorix, the falling of the sky was the only thing they ever feared, not battle, not death, not captivity.

Collins was a devout man, who practised his religion in a practical way. Where there was want, he believed in charity, and extended it generously. He visited the sick, and upheld the authority of his bishop, Macdonnell of Kingston, when the latter was opposed by an apostate priest, one O'Grady, who, in retaliation, refused baptism to Collins's infant son. To compound matters, Macdonnell, as the first Roman Catholic bishop in Upper Canada, felt duty bound to support the civil authorities, almost come weal or woe. From the same authorities Collins met nothing but woe.

He was a man of his times. He drank whiskey and ale, and made merry in good company with his friends. Take the very human picture of Collins announcing the birth of his only son, in the *Canadian Freeman* of 4 August 1831:

Birth.—In this town, on the 28th ult., the lady of the Editor of the *Freeman* of a son and heir.—Just as we had disposed of the old and new Reptile Bands, and their respective leaders Gurnet and Mackenzie, and put our paper to Press last week, the young Prince of Tyrone, FRANCIS PHELIM O'NEILL COLLINS, made his appearance with clenched fist, as if to grasp the sword of his great ancestor, and exhibiting as stern & independent a brow as that of the old Milesian Chief himself. The boy looks like the son of a *Freeman*—his arm seems admirably shaped for the defence of liberty, with a pair of legs to which nothing but a Highland kilt could do sufficient justice. When he ripens to maturity (if such be the will of Heaven) we trust he will show, that altho' a Canadian by birth, he has too much Milesian blood in his veins ever (like Gurnet of the *Courier*) to become a cringing sychophant and prostrate hireling to an official party—or, (like Mackenzie of the *Advocate*) the crawling degraded tool of any vile, canting, hypocritical and treacherous faction—but (like the father before him) resist, on the one hand, the tyranny of men in power, and on the other, oppose the march of fanaticism, hypocrisy, and false patriotism—the two great plagues of this his native country—the former of which visited the land, with terrific effect, during the late administration—and the latter, under the Ryersonian saddlebag religio-political junta, is now spreading its baleful influence all over the face of the country, and, like the locusts of Egypt, threatening destruction to the very verdure of the soil.

Collins travelled extensively throughout Upper Canada, attending meetings, reporting courts, through all seasons of the year when parliament was not in session. He reported everything of moment, and much that was not. His vignettes of everyday life are a rich heritage, bequeathing pictures of an era in Canada that was formative of a great and independent nation. He survived forty-five weeks' imprisonment in the common jail of York, with his spirit undaunted, emerged unscathed from the cholera plague of 1832, and was planning a new business establishment and the resumption of his career as a parliamentary reporter when he was stricken in the second epidemic two years later.

The word vigour has been aptly applied to the way he carried out his editorial duties. He had a high concept of the functions of a free press, uncommitted to parties or factions, and yet could poke fun at "the vanity of editors." To trace his writings from 1825 to

1834 is to observe his growth in maturity, a reflection in itself of the growing maturity of the colony of Upper Canada and of its capital. When he first began reporting the Debates in the House of Assembly, in 1819, many of its members were unlettered, unable even to sign their own names. Fifteen years later, this was no longer the case. The reform movement of 1818 had few supporters, fewer still after the banishment of Robert Gourlay and the Family Compact's vengeance upon his friends.

Later* in these chronicles are reproduced extracts from the *Freeman*, for each of the nine years of its existence. Collins gives his views on education, constitutional reform, corruption, penal reform, banking, parliamentarians, roads, railways and canals, public health and medical care, pollution and prostitution. They will help the reader form an independent judgment of the man and his times. These are the *ipissima verba* of the *Canadian Freeman*. Francis Collins was that Canadian free man.

*See pp. 120-34.

The *Canadian Freeman*

THE *Canadian Freeman* newspaper ran for nine years, from 1825 to 1834. The surviving file is broken, containing only one issue for 1825, none for 1826, eight for 1827, and then as follows: 36 (1828), 5 (1829), 26 (1830), 49 (1831), 29 (1832), 23 (1833), and 2 (1834). Advertisements indicated that it was probably first issued on 7 June 1825. The last surviving issue is dated 24 July 1834. Thus, of 457 known weekly issues, only 179 remain, occupying less than a 100-foot spool of microfilm.*

On one point past and present historians agree. The *Freeman* was technically well produced. The actual printing—given the equipment of the day, the quality of the paper and an uncontrollable humidity factor—was professional. Francis Collins and his brother John had learned their trade well in Newry. The frontispiece of the Journals of the Legislative Assembly for 1829 is a striking example of their style of execution.

It is worth stressing that the *Freeman* was handset from case. In other words, each letter of each word, each space between each word, and each punctuation mark were set by hand. Line by tedious line was hand-placed on a compositor's stick, transferred to a flat stone or metal surface, arranged in columns, with column rods between each, made up, justified, locked in an iron chase

---

*From a total of some twenty newspapers in the Canadas in 1825, when Collins founded the *Canadian Freeman*, the growth of the press and its offshoots has continued to the point where, in March 1979, the Task Force on Canadian Unity (co-chairmen: Jean-Luc Pépin and John P. Robarts) was able to report: "Canadians can now select their information from the following sources: 60 private and 60 CBC and affiliated TV stations; a total of 228 daily newspapers; over 500 community, ethnic and weekly newspapers; 411 private French and English AM and FM radio stations; and 55 CBC English and French AM and FM radio stations."

using quoins and wooden furniture, gingerly tested for solidity, and ever so carefully lifted and carried to the printing press, where again the chase was locked in position, the type inked by hand roller, a sheet of paper placed on top, an impression made, and with one swift motion the paper with its wet printed surface was stripped away.

For the reverse side of the paper, the entire process had to be repeated. Following that, the completely printed sheet was folded by hand, made up in bundles, and delivered, usually by the "printer's devil" or apprentice, doubling as newsboy, to shops and individual subscribers.

Then the whole procedure had to be done in reverse, chase to stone, type to case, letter by letter, space by space, punctuation mark by punctuation mark, all done by hand. This process is known as "dissing," and to watch an expert compositor diss is to see the human hand move with almost unbelievable speed, in a constant flicking action, as each letter is returned to its individual alphabet box in the case. It is said, though what truth there may be in it is conjectural, that William Bonney, otherwise known as "Billy the Kid," owed his expertise in the quick drawing of his left firearm to his apprenticeship in a printing office, dissing type.

In Toronto, in the 1820s and 1830s, Francis Collins not only reported the news with his "eagle quill" in shorthand, but himself, week after week, composed his editorials "direct from case," without first committing them to paper with pen and ink. Only one who has set from case can realize the tremendous mental effort required to keep a thought intact through such a process. "Follow your copy, even if it flies out the window!" never applied to Collins. His copy was in his head. All in all, it was a tremendous feat, and testimony to his accomplishment has been given by many contemporaries. The odd lapse in style and construction can readily be understood in these circumstances. Where there is a peculiar turn of phrase or grammatical awkwardness, the explanation may lie in the surmise that as a boy Collins used Irish, or was acquainted with its usage, and in later years, when rushed, applied its more rigid rules of grammar to express a thought in the freer flowing English.

Reporting the Debates

THE first surviving issue of the *Canadian Freeman* for 1827, that dated 18 January, deals at length with the subject of parliamentary reporting, and since these are Collins's own words, they deserve reproduction. They give the views of Canada's first professional parliamentary reporter, and tell something of the man himself:

> *Reporting.* We promised to revert to this subject, so important to the political interests of this Colony, and we regret that our time and limits prevent us from doing it justice. It will be seen by the debate on that question that the House, by a sweeping majority, have denied all encouragement to a reporter the present session. Whence comes this sudden change? The Attorney General and his *"ten"* have been uniform in endeavouring to suppress reporting for the last six years, and no blame to them; for every independent man in Upper Canada would disapprove of their measures in general, if they obtained a fair account of them. But what can the patriots say —what can some of the Gourlayites say, who voted away the money of their constituents for the last six years, at the rate of from £150 to £250 a year, for a service which is now so unnecessary that they would not even give the trade price for the printing work—the price of last session, to have it done gratis? Must it not make them appear most ridiculous in the eyes of their political opponents and of the country? Will the free and independent electors of Upper Canada be guided by such men? We hope not—we trust the good sense of the people will cause them to take such measures as will prevent any man, who voted away their money for reporting for six years, and on the seventh says it is an unnecessary service, from ever taking a seat again in the Assembly of this Province, and we shall be very free in pointing them out and their motives too, in due time, "so that the country may know them." We shall show the House of Assembly

that the *Freeman* is as much beyond their control as he is beyond the control of the Executive, so long as he knows how to keep within the bounds of the law... There was but one Reporter in Upper Canada unaided by Executive patronage—that Reporter was the Editor of the *Freeman*, who had exhausted his scanty means and embarrassed himself last winter in discharging that arduous duty by order of the House, and in furnishing a large number of his papers to the same order. Did he ever receive any remuneration? Not a farthing. The House, it is true, voted it, but the Executive, with a high and oppressive hand, retained it. Was this the time then for Mr Thompson... the talented *medalled* and highly patronized Editor of the *Kingston Herald* to expect that the *Freeman* would exhaust himself another year to fill the columns of the *Herald* and amuse his readers gratis? Was this the time for the Gourlayites to refuse their support to the *Freeman*? Was this the time, we ask an enlightened public, for a majority of the House to refuse encouragement to a faithful Reporter, who had exhausted his means by their order, and was reeling, as it were, under an Executive stab (for stab we must call it) —was this the time, we say, for that House whose head the *Freeman* shielded when no public voice was lifted for it effectually in Upper Canada, to strike him to the earth? Was it manly—was it honorable—was it just? No—we appeal even to our enemies, if greater injustice was ever done by a legislative body. We have never asked the patronage of the House—we have endeavoured to merit it, but we would disdain to ask it... We want no favour from the House, nor do we wish to take advantage of the trade; but if we have to perform a most arduous and expensive duty, as we did last year, in reporting the debates, and that the trade, as they did last year, take advantage of our labours, we contend that we have a right to compensation from some quarter, which we can never get from an increased circulation so long as such patriots as Mr Thompson have a free privilege of copying our reports; and those who have refused us this compensation, are either wholly unacquainted with the principles of justice, or have not given the case due consideration.

Collins went on to contrast the report by Stanton, then King's Printer, of a speech by a James Wilson, abbreviated to a mere stick of seven lines, and his own shorthand report of the same gentleman's speech that contained seventy-three columnar lines.

Mr Stanton is not capable of taking down the above speech; but if he were, dare he publish it in the *Gazette*? We say no. Is it not in the recollection of every man in York that when we reported for Dr Horne, his Excellency called up both the Dr and the Attorney General, who met together in the audience chamber, and that his Excellency would not allow the debates to be published in the Gazette at all, or in the same sheet with it, so that Dr Horne was obliged to publish a separate sheet to give the debates? Why does his Excellency admit them now? Because Mr Stanton carves them to suit his palate; and, strange to say, the patriot Thompson of Frontenac, who opposed all encouragement to the *Freeman*, as a competent reporter, imposes on his readers, as Editor, by republishing the foul, partial, and garbled report of the proceedings from the U.E. Loyalist, when the *Freeman* will not slave to gratify his penury and his readers' thirst for information!!! We are now speaking of Mr Thompson as Editor, and we intend to say a little more about him as soon as convenient . . .

Now what does the great Lord Erskine say, in a public letter on this business, before whose name the Attorney and his friends must sink into comparative insignificance? Lord Erskine, like an honest man, & an enlightened statesman, speaks as follows:

"Indeed I cannot conceive a more difficult or painful exertion of the human faculties, than that by which the proceedings in Parliament are generally preserved; and so far from being disposed to *peevish criticisms*, upon their imperfections, I have always thought that where malice, or undue partiality, could not be fairly attributed to them, *they were entitled to the utmost encouragement, and indulgence.* It would be a *wretched blank* in our history, and might in the end be *fatal to our liberties* if they were prohibited, or should fall into disuse. Shorthand, in its perfection, is a most rare talent."

Look to this, Mr Attorney, and think of the *"encouragement and indulgence"* you have given to this art for the last six years, by loading those who profess it, and who have practised it with advantage to the country, with the most unqualified abuse, shielded as you were, under the privilege of an Assembly in which, had justice been done you, you would never have been allowed to take your seat. Look to this, ye patriotic majority, who denied your aid to a stenographer, at a time when he was almost reduced to beggary by your means and by the oppressive measures of Sir Peregrine Maitland! Had Mr Attorney General or his friends any idea of the magnitude of the science they were endeavouring to suppress? Had Mr Thompson, the medalled Editor of the Kingston Herald, any idea of the *"painful exertion of the human faculties"* — (an exertion of which he was never capable)—when he refused it the slightest remuneration? Had Mr David Jones any idea of it when he was making his dull and *"peevish criticism"* upon it? No—their minds were not sufficiently lofty for such conceptions; but the great Erskine was the man who was capable of forming a correct idea of it. Let the patriots of Upper Canada, then, look to Lord Erskine's noble sentiments, and blush for their conduct—Let Sir Peregrine Maitland look to them, and blush for his treatment of the *Freeman* by withdrawing the reward of his labours—and if we cannot arraign him in this life for unjustly depriving us of our lawful wages, we hope to be able to arraign him before the bar of Divine Justice in the next.

Even in adversity, Collins showed his sense of humour, laughing both at himself and at others, as the following quotation from the same issue exemplifies:

As the election is approaching we anticipate, at last, some loud spouting, and having got through our share of the public accounts, we shall devote a few days to the use of our shorthand quill to lay the facts before the public, and allow the expense to be added to his Excellency's £113 10s. to be settled between his Excellency, the House, and ourselves, about the time that Fox agreed to settle with his creditors—either on the day of judgment or the day after.

The settlement of accounts between Maitland and Collins on the specified date will be followed with interest.

The Mortification of Maitland

IEUTENANT-Governor Sir Peregrine Maitland and his executive council had sought to strangle the *Canadian Freeman* by denying Collins his just wages. They miscalculated. The *Freeman* survived, and Collins turned the tables neatly on his oppressors, never letting them forget the injustice, and never letting the public forget it either. His was not the only case to which he turned his attention, however, as can be witnessed in his indictment "Encouragement of Literature and the Arts in Upper Canada under the administration of Sir Peregrine Maitland," in the issue of his newspaper for 8 February 1827. It is sad reading.

CLASSICS AND MATHEMATICS

Some of the ablest classical and mathematical scholars in this Province are spinning out a wretched thread of existence in teaching School, at a hire below that of the common labourer . . .

PAINTING

No person, professing this fine art, and looking to it for a living, could exist in the atmosphere of Upper Canada.

MUSIC

The same may be said with respect to this delightful science . . .

SCULPTURE AND STATUARY

In looking for the most remote appearance of any thing in this line here, we are obliged to make the common legal return—"non est inventus."

ENGINEER DRAWING

Upper Canada can boast of one of the first Engineer Draftsmen on this continent, Valentine Gill, Esq. The commissioners of Internal Navigation, after affording him some little employment, bestowed their further patronage upon him by accepting from him, *as a present*, one of the finest Maps in Upper Canada, which cost the artist immense labour and expense. The House of Assembly, finding that the artist was in indigent circumstances, voted him £40 for the execution of this map, and for his expenses in attending various sittings of the commissioners of Internal Navigation; but His Excellency, good and liberal soul! retains this pittance, and our poor artist is obliged to make a living for his family by digging in his garden in the village of Dundas!

STENOGRAPHY

There is but one tolerable Stenographer in Upper Canada, and the House of Assembly, for the last few years, voted him from £70 to £100 a year for reporting their proceedings, for the information of the country. His Excellency, after paying this item for *four years*, withheld it last year, after the Reporter had discharged this arduous duty, and without giving him any previous notice, with a view to crush the exercise of this rare science. This arbitrary and decisive step on the part of the Executive, shook the nerves of our Assembly-men in such a manner that they instantly turned round, in the face of five or six years' practice, and the present session refused the Stenographer as much public aid as would enable him to purchase pen, ink, and paper. He is now obliged to resign the duties of his profession and turn himself to other pursuits for a living.

PRINTING

This noble art, which has shed the rays of knowledge over the mind of man, and rescued it from original darkness—this beautiful science which is cultivated with the utmost veneration in all free countries, and under every liberal government, in Upper Canada is prostrated even to the dust of the earth . . .

Then there appears the following:

PUBLIC NOTICE

WHEREAS, £113 10s. having been voted to me by the House of Assembly last session, for four months' labour in reporting the debates, and for 45 newspapers a week, furnished by order of the House, during the session, this is to certify that the said sum of £113 10s. has been withheld from me up to this date, in a most unjust and arbitrary manner, by His Excellency Sir Peregrine Maitland, and I therefore call publicly on the House of Assembly, in the face of the country, either to obtain for me the said £113 10s. out of the public funds, or to pay the same out of their own pockets, as they, in their wisdom, may deem meet.

F. COLLINS
York, Feb. 3, 1827

By this stage Collins was reporting court cases at various assizes, many of which were published at length in the *Freeman*. On 8 November 1827 he wrote: "The *Freeman* can now boast of a subscription list, in the town of York, equal, if not superior, to any other journal ever published in it."* Nor was his editorial interest narrowly confined to Upper Canada. On 6 December, commenting on Dalhousie's refusal to approve the choice of Louis Joseph Papineau as Speaker of the Assembly in Lower Canada, he wrote plainly: "If Lord Dalhousie be not shortly removed from the Government of Lower Canada, and some more conciliatory character put in his stead, God only knows where all this business will end."

By now Collins had thoroughly aroused Maitland, Attorney-General John Beverly Robinson, and the rest of the Family Compact. They determined to take action through the courts, and each weekly issue of the *Freeman* was microscopically examined for grounds on which prosecution could be launched. One of the

---

*That the *Canadian Freeman*, then in its second year, was well on its way to becoming widely read throughout Upper Canada, can be evidenced from a notice on 11 October 1827, giving the following list of agents who distributed the paper: C. Culver, Niagara; J. Williamson, Stoney Creek; A. McDonnell, Guelph; R. Mullen, Hamilton; W.J. Sumner, Nelson; S. Daniel, Toronto; L. Stiles, Coburg; John Smith, Port Hope; G. Millward, Kingston; and A. McDonnell, Alexandria.

prerequisites of successful prosecution was proof of publication, tracing a newspaper back to its publisher. This required production of marked copies, showing them to have been received from Collins's printing establishment. The process extended over weeks and months, as can be seen in the *Freeman* files in the Public Archives of Canada, where one of the few surviving issues for 1827 carries the handwritten notation "recd. from Collins's Boy" and the signature "—King." When successful prosecution eventually came over a year later, instead of King, an informer named Wilmot was used to prove publication.

Scarcely a month went by without Collins chronicling the misdeeds of Maitland and his administration. On 28 August 1828, in a sub-leader, he wrote:

Good News, if true.—It has been currently reported in town for several days past that His Excellency Sir Peregrine Maitland is about to quit this colony for Halifax, in order to succeed Sir James Kemp as Lt. Governor of Nova Scotia. We hope this piece of information may turn out to be true, because we think it will prove beneficial to this Province to be relieved from the burthen of a torpid and nerveless administration. Some sycophantic addresses emanating altogether from a set of grovelling place-hunters have flattered Sir Peregrine by alluding to the great advantages which the people of Upper Canada have reaped from his administration. Now as we are wholly unacquainted with the benefits accruing from Sir Peregrine's administration, and as we do not like to speak hard of any man behind his back, we would like to ask Sir Peregrine himself, or any of his supporters, while he is yet on the spot, what he has done for Upper Canada during the last ten years that he has held the reigns of our colonial government—or rather that they have been held for him by Dr Strachan and J.B. Robinson? This is coming to the point—what good has emanated from Sir Peregrine Maitland, of his own free will and desire to serve the colony? We know of nothing. We do not want to asperse Sir Peregrine, although his conduct in depriving us of £113 10s. was oppressive, nay cruel in the extreme—but we must say that instead of conferring benefits on the colony, in our opinion, his own sluggish inactivity and the illiberal, unjust, and detestible policy of his unprincipled advisers, marred it[s] prosperity in the last ten years. It is said by some that

Sir Peregrine is a good soul as ever lived, but that he has had bad advisers . . . but leaving the evil policy of his advisers out of the question, where is his individual goodness? Upper Canada is one of the finest agricultural countries in the world. Sir Peregrine has presided over it for the tenth part of a century—has he established an Agricultural Society, an Horticultural Society, or any other Society for the good of the country? Has he given the slightest encouragement to trade or manufactures? Has he expended a shilling to patronise the arts and sciences? Has he not, on the contrary, most foully endeavoured to crush that noble art, *stenography*, from which the literary world has reaped such signal benefits, by depriving the Editor of the *Freeman* of £113 10s. after it was three times voted to him, by the House of Assembly, for services in that line? Have the tradesmen of York benefitted as much by Sir Peregrine in ten years, as they did in one night from the fancy ball given by Mr Galt and Judge Willis? Sir Peregrine is a good man—but who knows any thing about his goodness? Has he not avoided the circles of society, and shut himself up, for nine months of the year, in Stamford Lodge, living at an expense little above a common farmer, and wholly regardless of what was going on throughout the colony? . . . That the departure of Sir Peregrine, then, is a blessing to this colony, cannot, we think, for a moment be disputed; but poor Nova Scotia, we pity you. If Sir Peregrine is to be your Governor, what will become of your Agricultural and Horticultural Societies, matured by the wisdom, the enterprize, and the liberality of your former Governors, and now famed throughout the colonies? What will become of your unanimity, your enterprize, and public spirit?

On 2 October the *Freeman* joyfully confirmed the news of Maitland's impending removal, adding: "We do not know whether he will have the conscience to call and pay us our £113 10s. before he goes; if so we will wish the Novascotians luck of their bargain." A week later there appeared an extract from *The London Gazette* officially promoting the Lieutenant-Governor of Nova Scotia to Governor-in-Chief "of the Provinces of Lower and Upper Canada, Nova Scotia, New Brunswick, and the Island of Prince Edward," transferring Maitland to Halifax, and announcing the appointment of Major General Sir John Colborne as Lieutenant-Governor of Upper Canada. Thus was the stage set for Maitland, leaving office and departing Upper Canada, to sanction, as one of his last acts, institution of court proceedings against Francis Collins, whose just wages, two years earlier, he had cruelly withheld, and from whose editorial pen he had for so long suffered mortification and public humiliation.

The Willis Affair

TO put the trial of Collins in perspective, reference must be made to another figure, Judge John Walpole Willis (1793-1877), whose single year in Canada before his dismissal from office in June 1828 was instrumental in bringing the machinations of Lieutenant-Governor Maitland and the Family Compact to the public's attention. Willis had a poor opinion of John Beverly Robinson, the Attorney-General. What Robinson, in turn, thought of Willis, can be gleaned from his actions in helping to bring about his dismissal.

Willis was a threat to the governing oligarchy. He had been appointed one the of three judges of the Court of King's Bench in 1827 —the right man for the right job, but at the wrong time. He was not a member of the Compact and was determined to make the judiciary an independent branch, no longer subservient to the whim or wish of the executive council or Lieutenant-Governor. At the Spring Assizes of 1828, he was presented with an opportunity to do so courtesy of Francis Collins. It was an extraordinary scene.

On 10 April that year the executive council had moved openly against the *Canadian Freeman*, and Collins was indicted on two charges of libel. He had accused Maitland of "partiality, injustice and fraud" in not paying over the money voted to him by the House of Assembly, and had made certain references to the Solicitor-General, Henry John Boulton, respecting his conduct over a duel fought in 1817 between Samuel Peters Jarvis and John Rideout, that had resulted in the latter's death. On 11 April, two other prosecutions were instituted against Collins, a total of four in two days. It was not difficult to see how the land lay.

Collins immediately rounded on his accusers, and there followed a court scene that, for high drama, has few parallels in Canadian jurisprudence. It began innocuously. The following account is taken from the *Freeman* of 17 April 1828:

> "May it please your Lordship, I have a motion or two to make in Court, if your Lordship will say that I, not being a lawyer, am in order in so doing," said Collins.
> "Most certainly," replied his Lordship, "step forward that the Court may hear you." Francis Collins then stepped up to the Council-table and said, "My Lord, I am the humble conductor of a public press [the *Canadian Freeman*] in this town—I have come forward to accuse his Majesty's Attorney General with vindictiveness and foul partiality in the discharge of his duty as prosecuting officer for the Crown . . . "

Collins then outlined the charges he wished to make. The judge remarked that if the Attorney-General had acted as Collins had stated, then "he had very much neglected his duty." To which Attorney-General Robinson retorted:

> "I think, my Lord, I know my duty as well as any Judge on the Bench—and this is the way I have always acted and always will act, as long as I am prosecuting officer for the Crown."
> Judge Willis—"Then, sir, if you know your duty, you have neglected it—you have always acted improperly, and as you say you will continue to do so, I shall feel it to be my duty, holding his Majesty's commission as Judge on this Bench, to make a representation on your conduct to his Majesty's Government."

Robinson sat pale-faced, and the judge told Collins to go before the Grand Jury and prefer his complaints. J.C. Dent continues the story in these words:

> . . . these instructions he followed without a moment's unnecessary delay. He appeared before the Grand Jury, and charged H.J. Boulton and J.E. Small with being accessory to murder in the killing of young Rideout. He next laid a charge of rioting against S.P. Jarvis and six of the other persons [Peter McDougal, James King, John Lyons, Charles Richardson, Charles Howard, Charles Baby, and Henry Sherwood, Esqs.] who had figured as defendants in the action brought by Mackenzie. The Grand Jury speedily returned a

true bill against Boulton and Small. Both these gentlemen were then in Court with their gowns on. They were immediately put under arrest, and they so remained until late in the afternoon, when Judge Willis, upon the application of Mr Macaulay, admitted them to bail. As Jarvis had been tried for the offence and acquitted, shortly after the duel in 1817, the Grand Jury now returned "No bill" as to him. On the following Monday a true bill was returned by the Grand Jury against the seven persons charged with riot. They were promptly arrested and held to bail.*

Small was eventually acquitted, and the "type rioters" were found guilty. Dent records that Judge Willis was very lenient and sentenced them to a nominal fine of five shillings each, citing as justification the heavy damages already awarded to William Lyon Mackenzie in a prior civil action. All this had an effect on Attorney-General Robinson, who deemed it prudent not to proceed further with three of the charges against Francis Collins; on the fourth charge Collins was acquitted.

Yet this was far from the end of the concerted attempt to defame Collins. Indeed, Robinson's decision not to proceed with three of the charges against him set in train the events which culminated in his prosecution and sentencing at the Fall Assizes in the same year. By that time Maitland had arbitrarily removed Willis from the bench, and Robinson had a free hand. It was later held by the home government that, although Maitland had the authority to dismiss Willis, he had exercised it improperly.

With Willis gone, Collins had no hope of warding off the second assault made upon him with all the ferocity at the command of Robinson's "native malignancy."

---

*J.C. Dent, *The Upper Canadian Rebellion*, Vol. I (Toronto: C. Blackett Robinson, 1885), p. 198.

Vengeance for the Family Compact

THE attack on Collins was two-pronged: through the courts and through the government-controlled press. Maitland and Robinson had chosen to attack through the courts. The first indictments had been preferred as early as April 1828, but it was not until 25 October that the legal net was closed. Meanwhile, the more virulent newspaper supporters of the Family Compact set out to destroy Collins's personal reputation. The lead was taken by the Perth *Independent Examiner*. Its vehemence roused Collins to fury and satire, and in truth, Stewart, the newspaper's editor, did future generations a service by making Collins give a few biographical details that otherwise might have remained shrouded for all time. Here is Collins at his best pitch, writing in the *Freeman* of 18 September 1828:

> The *"immaculate villain"* who conducts the Perth volcano, says *he* "shall support the colonial government in every act." What support, in the name of common sense, can the colonial government receive from such a low, contemptible blackguard? Is it by calling his brother editors "patriotic villains!—immaculate villains!—unprincipled slanderers!—rascals! scoundrels!" &c. that this *Bombastes Furioso* of Perth is going to support the colonial government? If this be the way Sir Peregrine's administration is to be supported, we can supply His Excellency's advisers with any number of fish-women they may desire, who can be hired cheaper, and will be much more capable of editing a paper than either Stewart or M'Farlane.* But as Mr Stanton† has not defiled the columns of his paper with the *lava* from Stewart's volcano, we take it

*James Macfarlane was publisher of the *Kingston Chronicle*.

†Robert Stanton, the King's Printer, was publisher of the *Upper Canada Gazette*.

for granted that the government party are ashamed of such advocates.

Brimstone Stewart says he is an Irishman as well as the Editor of the *Freeman*. We are sorry for it, because it goes to establish an opinion already too prevalent in this country—namely, that when an Irishman is a blackguard, he is the greatest blackguard in the world. He claims acquaintance, too, with the Editor of this paper at home, and charitably insinuates that he is a *"refugee,"* who had to run away from Ireland to escape the gallows. Stewart's malice, however, has here over-reached itself, and can only serve to expose his own ignorance, and the hideous malignity of his heart—for the man who commits crime in Ireland is as liable to punishment in Canada as if he had remained at home. The Editor of the *Freeman* is well known in this colony—it is a public thing that he had the honor to be proprietor of a most respectable opposition newspaper in Ireland, and to grapple with, and suffer persecution from, the corruptest minister that ever disgraced the British cabinet (Castlereagh— a *Stewart*, too, who afterwards cut his throat—we hope his namesake in Perth will not follow the example)—that he was, in fact, at home just what he is here—a real *radical printer*—and a fearless advocate for the cause of freedom and independence. He has neither changed his name, his principles, nor his profession—and here he stands upon British ground, at the defiance of Stewart, or any other cringing sycophant in existence . . . Let Brimstone Stewart, then, take his *flagellum* in his hand, and go back to teach the A.B.C.—as a public writer he can do nothing in this colony. But before he goes, we would give him the advice offered to Sir Neal O'Donnell by Watty Cox—namely, to call his friends and physicians together, and hold a consultation in order to ascertain whether he is an *idiot* from intemperance or by birth.

The *Freeman* of 30 October 1828 carried the following report of Collins's trial, under the heading "Liberty of the Press in Upper Canada":

On Saturday last, the Editor of the Canadian *Freeman* was put on his trial for a libel upon the Administration of justice, a libel against Judge Hagerman, a libel against the Attorney General, and a libel against the Solicitor General, in the following paragraph:—

"*York Assizes.*—Our Assizes commenced here on Monday last, and the Attorney and little Boulton have put their heads

The Canadian Freeman *of 6 November 1828, with the first report of the "native malignancy" trial.*

together again on Tuesday, to see if they can do anything in
the way of *libel*. On that morning the Attorney General called
upon the Editor of the *Freeman* to take his trial upon one of the
cases of libel held over since last assizes. The Editor, who
pressed the Attorney to trial last court, when his counsel had
been brought to town at a heavy expense, by express, rose and
said that he was not ready for trial, neither of his counsel being
in court, and that from the undetermined manner in which
the Attorney General spoke last assizes, he did not expect that
proceedings would be followed up. As he had not been arraigned, however, he said he would traverse the indictment.
The Attorney General, with a view of bringing us to trial un-
prepared, first rose, and stated an open palpable falsehood in
Court—namely, that we had been arraigned last assizes.
When we contended to the contrary, to the satisfaction of the
court, the Attorney in his native malignancy, took till next
day (yesterday) to hunt up authorities to see if he could force
us to trial without the privilege of traverse, contrary to the
universal practice of the court. This he attempted to shew
yesterday, and our old *customer* Judge Hagerman was in
favour of the measure. Mr Robert Baldwin, in our behalf,
stated that he was taken by surprise—that he thought from
the observations of the Attorney General last Assizes, these
cases were quashed—such was the opinion of Mr Rolph,
leading counsel, and the defendant himself, and that as he did
not think the Attorney General would refuse the right to traverse, he was not prepared to reply to his argument against it.
The question is to be decided to-day; in the meantime we expect Mr Rolph here daily, and when he arrives, we shall show
the Attorney and little Boulton that we are not afraid to meet
them."

The preliminary statements in the above article were proved to
be correct, so far as that it was admitted the Attorney General had
stated, if not "an open palpable falsehood," at least that which was
untrue—that the defendant had traversed—and it was also admitted
and *ruled* by the Court, that the Attorney General was wrong in
afterwards denying the right to traverse. The evidence went to the
jury, they retired, and in some time afterwards sent out for *Johnson's
Dictionary*.* This was refused, and the Jury, after remaining out for

*Nobody on the jury knew the meaning of the word "malignancy."

five hours, returned with a verdict of *"Guilty of a libel upon the Attorney General."* Mr Justice Hagerman, who then presided, told the jury that this verdict could not be received—they must either bring in a verdict of guilty or not guilty; when the jury, contrary to their first verdict, and contrary to their oaths (as we humbly conceive) retired, and in five minutes brought in a general verdict of "GUILTY."

Messrs Rolph and Baldwin made 4 legal objections to this verdict, and the Court adjourned and took them into consideration.

Yesterday the Court determined (Mr Justice Sherwood and Mr Justice Hagerman presiding) that the legal objections made were of no weight, and sentenced the Editor to ONE YEAR'S imprisonment in the Common Gaol of the District, to pay a fine of £50 at the end of the imprisonment, to lodge bail, himself in £400, and two sureties in £100 each, for good behaviour for 3 years, and to stand committed until these conditions be complied with.

Messrs Rolph and Baldwin were Counsel for the defendant, and managed his cause with great ability.

Mr Allan Wilmot, in absence of Davy Stegman, was the informer, and the following names composed the Jury:—

William Davenish, John Hayden, Peter Lytle, Thomas Cosford, William Elliott, Daniel Knowles, Andrew A. Thompson, Thomas Walton, Jonathan Gates, John Richardson, Bradshaw McMurray, Duncan Kennedy.

A Public Meeting is called, by a hand bill, on Monday next at noon, in the public MARKET SQUARE, York to take this matter into consideration. In the meantime the FREEMAN stands committed, and occupies the old quarters of Colonels Coffin and Givens.

Collins in Jail

COLLINS was sentenced on 29 October and was immediately committed to York jail. Maitland, Robinson, Sherwood, Hagerman and their ilk were ecstatic. In her book *The Town of York 1815-1834*,* Edith Firth has included a letter written the next day by Sheriff Jarvis to W.D. Powell, which lays his feelings bare.

> ... yesterday that Precious Scoundrel Collins was brot up for Judgement in the libel case and he received the sentence of the Court as follows—a fine of fifty pounds—one years imprisonment, and Security for good behaviour, for three years, himself on 400£ & two surities of two hundred each—& to remain in prison until the fine be paid—I was passing at the time he was conveyed to Gaol, & could not resist the temptation of wishing him joy at the present termination of his unprincipled career. This morning Placards are up in all parts of the town calling a Public Meeting, in order to devise means to repel the attack that has been so unexpectedly made upon the great Bulwark of our liberties, and to shield a free Press from annihilation—I send you one of them—The Severity of the Sentence exceeds anything that was anticipated by him—indeed I verily believe that he and all his party had the presumption to imagine that no Judge would dare to visit him with punishment of any kind—McKenzie and that Prince of Liars Mr Carey looked very blank when the Sentence was pronounced—I have seen the Baldwins, Mr Rolph & the two Editors together since all bearing the appearance of great consternation ...

A better account of the official relief at "the present termination" of Collins's career as a crusader for reform could not be given.

*Edith G. Firth, *The Town of York 1815-1834* (Toronto: The Champlain Society, 1966).

However, in their eagerness to put an end to the *Canadian Freeman* by lodging its editor in jail, the Family Compact overlooked one factor, the character of Francis Collins himself. With his own experience to guide him, and the example of William Cobbett years earlier, between Saturday's trial and Wednesday's sentencing he made preparations to carry on publication of the *Freeman*, at whatever cost to himself, to his wife and family, and to his relatives. His brother John would be depended upon to supervise production of the paper in his spare time. John Carey, it may safely be assumed, would give a helping hand.

As each day passed, the groundswell of public opinion began to rise higher in favour of Collins. Robinson was hissed at in the streets.

Collins took to jail with him quill, ink and paper. He wrote, and what he wrote, he published. John Mitchel's *Jail Journal*, Raleigh's *History of the World*, Bunyan's *The Pilgrim's Progress*, and Wilde's *De Profundis*—some of the finest writing has been done within the confines of a jail.

One of the little remarked upon curiosities of Collins's trial was that throughout the hearing he himself was the reporter of record. He was still the only professional shorthand reporter in the colony and, though being the defendant on trial, recorded the entire proceedings. A week after his incarceration, he began to publish the trial's transcript in the *Freeman*. The issue of 6 November carries eight full columns and contains the speech of his defence counsel, John Rolph, it is believed in its entirety. Unfortunately the next week's issue has not survived. Only one witness was called by the Attorney-General, the informer needed to prove publication:

> *Allan Wilmot*, (the informer) sworn—Witness was in the employment of Mr Stegman, the merchant—his employer was a subscriber to the *Canadian Freeman*, and received it weekly. It generally came out on *Wednesday*. (As this was known to be a falsehood, it created a general laugh in court.) On looking to the paper witness then swore it came out on *Thursday*. (A laugh.) It was delivered by a boy in the employment of the Editor.
>
> Cross-examined by Mr Baldwin—Witness was a clerk with Stegman—did not know it was any part of his duty to become a common informer and to prosecute the Editor—was subpoenaed to

attend—Stegman was out of town at present—knew the paper to be the identical one delivered because he had a mark upon it—the name of witness and Matthew Keys, the boy who delivered it, were marked upon it—When the paper was delivered, witness left it down upon the desk and went to attend to his customers—thought it was impossible that the paper could be changed, as he soon afterwards put his name upon it, before many persons came in—could not swear positively that it was not changed as Edward Coates, a boy who attended the shop, came in.—Young Mr Sherwood soon afterwards came in and took it away. Before Stegman went away he gave witness directions to mark the *Canadian Freeman* newspapers.

Here the Attorney General closed his case. Mr R. Baldwin then said he hoped the Court would order a non-suit, as the Attorney General closed his case without reading the alledged libel. After some discussion, however, the Court took note of the objection and ordered the alledged libel to be read as follows:—*

The paragraph including the phrases "native malignancy" and "our old *customer*" were then repeated, following which came Rolph's address to the jury. It was a masterpiece, but in a lost cause:

Gentlemen, you are told that this is a simple prosecution against Francis Collins; but, open your eyes and see the blow which, under that pretence, is aimed against the Press.

The Press is the most powerful engine of the human mind. It diffuses knowledge far and wide. It is the press which discusses public measures and enlightens the public mind. It is the press which criticises the public conduct of public men, and which drags them from the recesses of courts and cabinets and holds them up before the tribunal of public opinion. It is the press which makes the common people too wise; and therefore, the press is hated by many rulers; and why? Because "they cannot bear the light, neither will they come to the light, because their deeds are evil!" Hence it always has been with such men a grand desideratum how this nuisance called the press can be put down or kept in a state of subjection. Various, indeed, have been the intrigues and the contrivances in the history of different countries for the accomplishment of this darling purpose; but Upper Canada, considering that we

Canadian Freeman, 6 November 1828.

form part of the freest Empire in the world, has perhaps been more fruitful of expedients than France or Spain or any other European power. And to the enduring honor of the *Canadian Freeman*, and his associates in the public ranks, be it ever spoken, they have risen superior to all fears and allurements in the discharge of a most important and, as you see this day, a very perilous duty . . .

Rolph went on to quote at length from "demi-official" and official organs, such as the Kingston *Herald* and the *Upper Canada Gazette*—example after example of "nasty, vulgar, scurrilous and most defamatory matter" published with impunity—and from Edmund Burke on the trial of John Wilkes. He carefully noted that "Mr Sherwood, a son of the learned judge, and a pupil of the learned Attorney General, was in attendance at Mr Stegman's," and that the Attorney General had been wrong in his facts. Questioning whether the jury would protect Collins, "who had the courage to maintain his rights," Rolph concluded:

Take away the salutary restraint of popular opinion, which affords so powerful an incentive to circumspection of conduct, and correctness in asserting, and you will open a sort of pandora's box upon the community in which you live—mistakes would multiply from the very impunity with which they would be committed. But when it is known that the Press is free to discuss and to censure those errors which threaten to grow into encroachments subversive of the rights of prisoners and the liberty of the subject, then is immediately awakened that spirit of caution and prudence in putting forward undue pretensions and questionable rights, which is only enjoyed in those happy countries where the Press is free, and where juries have virtue and courage enough to keep it so.

If Rolph thought for a moment that he was addressing a virtuous and courageous jury, he certainly did not know his men.

Meanwhile, Collins was locked up in York jail, suffering not only the usual privations but an additional burden. Jarvis, the Sheriff, was a Family Compact man, who, "at intervals, as his caprice directs, gives orders to the Gaoler to deny the prisoner the privilege of seeing any person, *even his wife and children*, for 24 hours at a time . . . " According to the custom of the era, prisoners were permitted visitors at all reasonable times and, had they the means, could "lodge" their families with them. (In present-day parlance, there were conjugal visiting rights and prisoners exercised them.) But Jarvis was not prepared to allow Collins any easement. Yet public opinion, and Collins's own pen, were to prove stronger, and within a matter of weeks the Sheriff capitulated.

Writing in the *Freeman* on 6 November, Collins reported the execution of a condemned murderer, one John Christie, who "met his fate with unusual firmness and composure." Then appeared the following paragraph:

> *The Gallows.*—This hideous instrument of death, which now stands in front of our lodgings, we hear is to remain a permanent spectacle of disgust for the good people of *Little* York, merely to save Mr Sheriff Jarvis the trouble of taking it down, which could be done by two labourers in half an hour! . . . The steps of the Gallows obstruct the passage into the Gaol, and when Mr Sheriff Jarvis told us he would have it removed and neglects to do so, we cannot but feel that it is kept there as an indignity to the friends of the *Freeman*.

Collins also reported the arrival of Sir John Colborne during the week to take up duty as Lieutenant-Governor on the departure of Maitland.

The term "packed" can be applied without qualification to the jury in Collins's trial.

> And there were other facts which had an ugly look. The defendant, as already mentioned, was a Roman Catholic; yet, out of a large and respectable population professing the same religious faith, not one was to be found on the panel, although at the Quarter Sessions, held a few days later, the number of Roman Catholics summoned to serve on juries was exceptionally large. The Sheriff who empanelled the jury was a political enemy of the accused. So was each individual member of the Grand Jury who found the true bill against him. So was the Attorney-General who prosecuted him. So were the two Judges who presided at the trial . . . It was no wonder that public meetings were held in some of the rural districts to protest against what was almost universally pronounced to be a tyrannical abuse of the process of the Courts.*

*Dent, op. cit., Vol. I, p. 208.

For weeks afterwards Collins published the names and nationalities of the jurymen in large type in his newspaper. There were two Americans, four Scots and five Englishmen; the twelfth was described as an Irishman. On 26 November, almost a month after his imprisonment, when Collins petitioned the new Lieutenant-Governor for relief, he was able to submit two affidavits and accompanying documents demonstrating the prejudice and ignorance of two members of the packed jury.

The petition of Francis Collins

York Gaol, Novr. 24th, 1828.

Sir,

I have the honor to acquaint your Excellency that I am the Editor of the Canadian Freeman now confined in this gaol on a charge of libel. I have addressed to your Excellency, at your office, the *Freeman* newspaper for the last three weeks containing a correct report of the proceedings on my trial, with a copy of the article declared to be libellous, in the hope that from your Excellency's very exalted character nothing more would be necessary to ensure the interposition of the Royal Prerogative on my behalf; but it is possible that they may not have reached your Excellency's hands. Had your Excellency perused these documents, I am certain you would concur in the general opinion that there is nothing libellous in the article upon which I am convicted, and that a London Editor could treat the Prime Minister of England with double the severity which I have applied to Mr Robinson, without the slightest risk of a prosecution.

As your Excellency, in your reply to the committee who addressed you in my behalf, alluded to that great palladium of our liberties "trial by jury," for which no person has more veneration than myself, I herewith submit to your Excellency two affidavits, which, I hope, will satisfy your Excellency that in my case that glorious privilege was exercised in mockery of justice. By one of these affidavits, your Excellency will perceive that *two* of the jurors on my trial were predetermined to convict me. By the other, your Excellency will see the deplorable ignorance of jurors in this country, when out of twelve men not one of them knew the meaning of the words "native malignancy," yet strange to say, they took it upon

The petition of Francis Collins to Sir John Colborne.

By one of these affidavits, your Excellency
will perceive that two of the jurors on my
trial were predetermined to convict me—
By the other, your Excellency will see
the deplorable ignorance of jurors in this
country, when out of twelve men not one
of them knew the meaning of the words
"native malignancy," yet strange to say, they
took it upon their consciences to declare them
"false, scandalous, and malicious".

Under all these circumstances, I hope
your Excellency will feel it compatible
with your duty and the ends of justice
to grant me immediate relief from
a sentence which, even by my political
enemies, is declared most unjust and oppressive.
It is said your Excellency came amongst us to
conciliate and allay the political animosities
of the colony, and your Excellency may rest
assured that the people of Upper Canada look
up to your determination in my case (as the
first that came before you) with intense anxiety.

I have the honor to be,
Your Excellency's very obt.
hum'ble servant,
Francis Collins.

His Excellency
Sir John Colborne, K. C. B.
&c. &c. &c.

their consciences to declare them "false, scandalous, and malicious."

Under all these circumstances, I hope your Excellency will feel it compatible with your duty and the ends of justice to grant me immediate relief from a sentence which, even by my political enemies, is declared most unjust and oppressive. It is said your Excellency came amongst us to conciliate and allay the political animosities of the colony, and your Excellency may rest assured that the people of Upper Canada look up to your determination on my case (as the first that came before you) with intense anxiety.

> I have the honor to be,
> Your Excellency's very obt. &
> Humble servant,
> Francis Collins.

His Excellency
Sir John Colborne, K.C.B.,
&c. &c. &c.

One of the deponents, Thomas Kenedy of the township of Scarborough, even accompanied his deposition with a testimonial to his honesty. The signatories to this testimonial were Henry Sullivan, John Baldwin, M. Scollard, Charles Keller, Robert Rutherford, and Alex Burnside. Kenedy, on oath, swore that:

> . . . he was in attendance, as a juror, at the late assizes of York, and that on the day that Francis Collins, Editor of the *Canadian Freeman*, was convicted of libel, before the trial this deponent had a conversation with Wm. Davenish, one of the jurors also in attendance at the said assizes, who said that if he, the said Wm. Davenish, would be called as a juror on the trial of him, the said Francis Collins, he *"would put it on to him,"* — giving the deponent to understand and believe that he, the said Wm. Davenish, was predetermined to convict the said Francis Collins be it right or wrong.

Kenedy deposed likewise in respect of Andrew A. Thompson, another member of the jury.

A second deposition, made out by Patrick Kenney of the town of York, related that:

. . . since the trial of Francis Collins, editor of the *Canadian Freeman*, for libel, he had several conversations with John Hayden, of the town of York, carpenter, one of the jury who convicted the said Francis Collins, in the course of which he, the said John Hayden, repeatedly told this deponent that the said Francis Collins was convicted on account of applying the words "native malignancy" to the Atty. General. And this deponent further saith that he, the said John Hayden, acknowledged that he did not at the time of giving this verdict, know the true meaning of the word *malignancy*, having sent out to the court from the jury room for Johnson's Dictionary for that purpose, which was refused—and that from the explanation given of the said word by one of the jurors, the said John Hayden was induced to believe it to be a much worse term than he had since found it to be on consulting Dictionaries, and, therefore, gave his voice for the conviction of him, the said Francis Collins, for which he has since expressed his regret.

Prejudice and ignorance were the weapons used to send Francis Collins to jail. They had also been used with success against him in Ireland.

After a delay of some weeks, Collins's petition was rejected by Sir John Colborne.*

---

*For a report of a committee of the House of Assembly on conditions in York jail, see Appendix Two, pp. 224-26.

Parliament and the Press

TURNED down by Colborne, Collins was advised to petition the Commons, where he was assured of support from the majority of the elected representatives. This he did, and the House agreed to consider his petition. Now the game would be played out in the open, according to Parliament's rules, with John Carey reporting the proceedings for the edification of the public and the benefit of posterity.*

A parliamentary committee was appointed to consider Collins's petition. In his cross-examination by the committee, Attorney General Robinson was asked the following question:

> On what authority is it, that persons are held to bail for good behaviour, before they have been convicted of the offences?

His reply contained a startling allusion:

> Mr McKean, a lawyer of eminence formerly Chief Justice, and afterwards Governor of Pennsylvania, in a charge delivered to the Grand Jury of the city and county of Philadelphia, on the 27 November 1797, after an exposition of the law relative to libels, informs them, "that a certain printer in that city, (meaning Cobbett, the publisher of *Porcupine's Gazette*) was, and long had been in the habit of offending against the law by the publication of scandalous, and malicious libels—that he had interfered and endeavoured to arrest the progress of this offender *by binding him over to be of good behaviour*, but that the printer in contempt of this recognizance, and in defiance of the authority of the law, persisted in his

---

*His report is to be found in the *Appendix* to the *Journal of the House of Assembly* for 1829, page 23.

mischievous course, and that the duty of arresting him now de-
volved on the grand jury, by whom alone the strong correctives
appearing to be necessary could be applied."

I cite this instance not because it is of so much weight as the
English authorities upon the same point, but because it may be
satisfactory to shew that our system of jurisprudence does not
sanction a more rigorous control over the evils of a licentious press
than has been exercised in another country where the freedom of
the press is often erroneously supposed to exist almost without control.

John Hayden, the contrite juror, was a most reluctant witness.
Three times he replied to questions, "I am not prepared to
answer." The transcript then continues:

QUESTION.—Did you not call upon Collins in Jail, and did you not
tell him that you were sorry for having found the verdict of "guilty,"
and that the finding was owing to your ignorance of the word
"malignancy"?

ANSWER.—I do not think proper to answer.

Hayden had chosen to wash his hands of the affair in public.

The two Justices, Sherwood and Hagerman, properly declined
to subject themselves to examination. However, the committee did
have before it Sherwood's charge to the jury, with the following
certifications attached to it:

I hereby certify, that I have taken down the above charge in shorthand, and that in substance it is perfectly correct.

(Signed) Francis Collins,
Stenographer

I hereby certify, that the above charge of Judge Sherwood, is in substance true.

(Signed) John Carey,
York,
9th March, 1829

The last five sentences in the charge indicate Sherwood's concept of his duty as an impartial judge:

In the next place the editor speaks of his "*old customer*," Judge Hagerman. Now, I view the expression "*customer*," a figurative allusion to the business of merchants, or mechanics, and it clearly implies that the editor of this paper, has made remarks upon this gentleman before, *as a retailer of calumny; but, in my opinion gentlemen, this editor is no petty retailer, but a wholesale retailer of calumny.* This is my opinion, gentlemen, and, as a Judge of this court, I have a right to express it. It is contended by some, that a judge has not the power to express his opinion in this way; but I contend that he has the power; a constitutional power to express his opinion on all matters that come before him—a power too that ought always to be exercised by a judge in the discharge of his duty; and I shall always give my opinion freely, where I think my duty calls me so to do. I think, gentlemen, that this is a libel; a gross and scandalous libel; but you can determine as you think proper; and whether you determine that it is a libel, or is not, I shall still have the same good opinion of you; as I know you will determine as you think right, and I have done my duty.

Also before the committee was a letter written to Colborne by Sherwood, giving the grounds for the severe sentence imposed on Collins, and concluding:

Taking all the circumstances of the case into consideration, Mr Justice Hagerman and myself deemed the sentence which we passed on the defendant, both proper and necessary, for the public good, and what the case itself required.

Colborne's reply to the Assembly's petition for clemency for Collins contained the following terse rejection:

. . . I regret exceedingly that the House of Assembly should have made an application to me, which the obligation I am under to support the laws, and my duty to Society, forbid me, I think, to comply with.

But the case of Francis Collins would not die. The following extract from the *Journal of the House of Assembly* for 12 March 1829 tells the outcome:

TO THE KING'S MOST EXCELLENT MAJESTY
Most Gracious Sovereign,
WE, Your Majesty's dutiful and loyal subjects, the Commons of Upper Canada in Provincial parliament assembled, humbly request your Majesty's most favourable consideration of the resolutions and documents accompanying this address, and humbly pray your Majesty to extend to Francis Collins the Royal clemency, by remitting the residue of his punishment—which act of mercy will be most acceptable to the people of this province, and be regarded by us as a fresh proof of Your Majesty's gracious disposition to consult the wishes and happiness of your people in all parts of your ample dominions. And that Your Majesty will be graciously pleased to lay a copy of the resolutions and accompanying documents before your Majesty's Parliament of the United Kingdom of Great Britain and Ireland.

MARSHALL S. BIDWELL
Speaker

Commons House of Assembly
12th March, 1829

On the question of passing the same, the House divided, and the Yeas and Nays were taken as follows:

YEAS—Messrs. Baldwin, Blacklock, Buell, Cawthra, Dalton, Ewing, Hornor, Ketchum, Kilborn, Lefferty, Lockwood, Lyons, McDonald, Mackenzie, Malcolm, Matthews, Perry, Peterson, John Rolph, Shaver, Smith, Thomson, James Wilson, & Woodruff —24.
NAYS—Messrs. Dickson, Henderson, Longley, Morris, Radenhurst, Samson, Terry, and Wilkinson—8.
The question was carried in the affirmative by a majority of sixteen . . .

In all, seventeen resolutions, with amendments, were debated and voted upon over the course of two days, of which a number dealing with freedom of the press are worthy of incorporation in the present chronicle.

For example, the tenth resolution, carried by a vote of 39 to 3, read:

> Resolved—That the punishment inflicted upon Francis Collins for the said libel, viz: "that he should be imprisoned for 12 months, pay a fine of £50 to the King, find sureties for his good behaviour after his liberation, for 3 years, himself in £400, and two sureties in £100 each, and stand committed till all those conditions should be complied with"—is, considering the state of the province and circumstances of the defendant, shamefully disproportioned to his offence,—subversive of the freedom of the press, under pretence of correcting its excesses; and destructive of the liberty of the subject, under pretence of punishing an offender.

The fifteenth resolution, carried 32 to 4, read:

> Resolved, that it is inconsistent with the liberty of the press, that a person should, before conviction, be called upon to find bail for good behaviour, upon so indefinite an offence as libel; and that the law under which such proceeding is justified in this province, is well objected to by Lord Ashburton in the following terms: "I never heard till very lately, that Attornies General, upon the caption of a man supposed a libeller, could insist on his giving securities for his good behaviour. It is a doctrine injurious to the freedom of every subject, derogatory from the old constitution, and a violent attack if not an absolute breach of the liberty of the press. It is not law, and I will not submit to it.

On the strict question of the legality of the imposition of the sentence, the eighth resolution, carried by 29 to 11, affirmed:

> Resolved—That it appears from the appended copy of the letter of Judge Sherwood to His Excellency, (marked E), that Mr Justice Hagerman alleged on the record to be libelled, did concern himself with Mr Justice Sherwood, in measuring the punishment of the defendant, thereby, without necessity for it, further violating the rule, that a man shall not be a judge in his own case.

Seven weeks before the end of his prison sentence, notice of the royal clemency reached York, and Collins was released without having to provide sureties and recognizances, as originally had been stipulated.

Before leaving the subject of parliament and the press, a further indication of the support the Assembly was prepared to give Collins should be noted. On 20 March, the House awarded the printing of its *Journals* to Collins, still in jail, the printing of the Appendix to be shared by Carey and Mackenzie. Robinson and Boulton, the Solicitor-General, later submitted accounts totalling £16 10s. as their fees for prosecuting Collins.

Collins Today

THE Canadian Catholic Historical Association in its 1938-39 Report carried an article on Francis Collins written by Rev. Brother Alfred,* in which he penned the following words:

> Strange to say, the name of Francis Collins seems to have been entirely lost among his own people in Toronto. No monument, no shaft, no tablet, not even an inscription marks his last resting place. He is numbered with the forgotten dead. Truly it can be said of him in the lines of Axel Munthe: "Not to the jubilant Capital of fame, but to the Silent Campo of oblivion death led the way. His sun had barely reached the height of mid-day when death overtook him."
>
> Francis Collins passed suddenly and tragically off the stage, but the drama in which he played a prominent and agonizing role in Upper Canada went on until it broke, unfortunately, in the tragedy of bloody rebellion three years after his untimely death. He slept on undisturbed, however, in his "narrow cell," under the shadow of the cross in old St Paul's cemetery on Power St., Toronto, though the clash of arms and the voices of angry men resounded over his quiet grave. His ideas and his ideals of civil government had finally triumphed, though he knew it not, and the Family Compact Regime was swept away forever.

Members of the Family Compact, however, are memorialized in full, in place and street names, throughout present-day Toronto. There is a Colborne Street, a Maitland Street and Maitland Place, a Robinson Avenue and a Robinson Street, two Sherwood Avenues, a Hagerman Street, a Boulton Avenue and a Boulton

---

*The Rev. Brother Alfred, F.S.C., LL.D., founder of De La Salle College, "Oaklands," Toronto, and of St Joseph's College, University of Alberta, Edmonton. The article may be found on pages 51-66 of the Report.

Drive. But the native Torontonian or inquiring visitor will search in vain for any Collins Court, Collins Place, Collins Street, or Collins Alley. New Street, where he printed and published the *Canadian Freeman*, "one door north of Market-square," has been renamed Jarvis Street. Caroline, the street on which he and his wife lived and reared their family, is now called Sherbourne.

At St Paul's Church, on the corner of King and Power Streets, there is no longer a cemetery. But, "fiat justitia," some day there will be a plaque, a street, a building, and on it the name of Canada's first professional debates reporter and martyr in the cause of freedom of the press.

The son of Francis Collins, in death, as with the father before him in life, was linked with the story of *Hansard* in Canada. *The Daily Globe*, forerunner of the *Globe and Mail*, in its issue of 11 May 1874, carried this formal death notice:

> On Saturday, the 9th instant, FRANCIS COLLINS, aged 42 years, only son of the late Francis Collins, Esq., of this city. R.I.P.
>
> The funeral will take place at 10 a.m. on Tuesday, 12th inst., from the residence of Mrs Scollard, 17 Breadalbane-st. Friends will accept this intimation.

On the *very same* page the *Globe* ran an editorial headed "A Canadian Hansard," fulminating against the outrageous recommendation of a parliamentary committee that an official report be established for the House of Commons in Ottawa. The argument against reporting parliament fully and openly still found favour in certain circles in Toronto, whose spokesman was the *Globe*:

> What is the object—to give the speeches of the leading men *in extenso*? No; this cannot be the object; for those speeches are given *in extenso* now by the newspapers. To give the speeches of little men *in extenso*? This is the only object that would be gained. But is this a desirable object? Who cares to load the shelves of the Parliamentary Library with twaddle to which nobody would ever refer? . . . How contemptible must be the egotism delighting in an enforced importance that is yet no importance . . .
>
> And now let us say one word as to the danger of such a scheme.

We tremble for the effect that would be produced if each member knew that his every word would be reported. Twaddle would then, like Tennyson's brook, "go on for ever," and Windbag would be evermore reminding the House of Aeolus when entreated by Juno to untie the Notus and his brethern, only it is not ships that would be submerged, but sense and time and mercy.

For good measure the *Globe* urged the adoption of the English system, pointing out that:

Mr Hansard is a private person who took it into his head to cut out the reports from the *Times*, and publish them in volumes . . .

And on practical grounds it observed:

. . . the Hansard sheets will not be out before three o'clock, by which time the country will have read the papers.

Forty-eight hours later the *Globe* destroyed its own argument about the promptness of the newspapers in reporting the debates, by carrying a report subheaded "Continuation of Monday's proceedings," being then two days late.

The *Globe* returned to the subject on 20 May with a second editorial denouncing the proposed establishment of a Canadian *Hansard.* "No man," wrote the *Globe,*

is less fit to judge of the report of a speech than the man who made it. This sounds a paradox, but it is an axiom of reporting experience. "I never said this. I never could have said it," is the cry frequently of an orator reading a verbatim account of what he said, done by a reporter with an ear and hand of infallible reliability. When an orator reads his own speeches in the coldness of common sense, and without the divine afflatus he felt when on his legs, it is like an appeal from Phillip drunk to Phillip sober.* There is a story told of a leading member of the great Tory party of Canada making a speech

---

*The reference to Phillip drunk versus Phillip sober was elucidated in 1977 by Grattan O'Leary. In his posthumous, captivating *Recollections of People, Press and Politics*, he identified the reporter as P.D. Ross of the Ottawa *Journal* and the orator as Sir John A. Macdonald. It has the ring of truth to it.

which seemed to the reporter to be anything but surcharged with wisdom. The reporter waited on the great man the next day, and said he wished to read the speech to him. "Good," cried the important politician, "that is the very thing I should like you to do. I'm glad you have not sent it off." The reporter had not proceeded many sentences when he was stopped by the orator, who cried, "I never said that." "I assure you you did," replied the reporter. "Well, go on," cried the ruler of men. When the reporter had proceeded to the length of a few more sentences he was again stopped, with the exclamation "I never said that." At last they decided to throw over the report, and to have the reporter take down a speech, dictated there and then. This was done, and when the reporter was leaving with a satisfactory speech delivered to the bare walls of the room, he was called back, and the orator, with a good deal of wit, said to him, "Look here, young man, when you come down to report a Cabinet Minister's speech again, don't get drunk!" The public got a cooked report, as we fear they will often get in the proposed *Hansard*. Now, what the public want to know is, what was done and said; they don't want what was meant to be . . . they want to see their members as they appear in the Commons, grand, massive, tawdry, or imbecile, as the case may be.

The *Globe*, however, saw some financial good for itself if the proposal succeeded.

The papers would not feel bound to go to great expense to secure a good report, as they do now, feeling bound to keep a record. The seventy-five or a hundred dollars a week spent on reporters, and a larger sum which we spend on telegraphing, would be in great part saved . . . .

Its parting shot was delivered in these words:

It is plain that the House is committed to a far larger and more costly undertaking than it imagines; that the end aimed at is not understood; that the means are ludicrously inadequate; and that while no good can certainly be calculated on as following on the ill-conceived enterprise, many evils will crowd into its wake. The character of Parliament will be lowered, for it cannot but be that men will speak not to persuade but to fill the columns of *Hansard*, and this could not fail to degrade the character of the House. The end of all the deliberations of that House is, and should be, an act, and this should be kept well in view. When it is not, compression, force, and dignity are thrown to the winds, and instead of legislators and counsellors we find ourselves face to face with a debating society, where men speak not because the country is in need of their advice—not because some error is to be exploded—not because a particular view ought to be pressed on the Government, but for the reporter . . . and the imaginary groper of the future seeking for political wisdom and the stimulating rush and glow of by-gone Demosthenic fire.

If that bygone editorialist could only see the host of "imaginary gropers of the future" in the Public Archives of Canada a hundred years later, day in and day out, diligently perusing the bound volumes of *Hansard* that he so opposed and sought to abort, he would be amazed at the error of his own soothsaying.

Three daughters were also born to Ann Moore and her husband. Mary, the eldest, died at the age of nine years, a day after her father's death in 1834; Margaret, the second daughter, became Mrs Finbar Hayes; and the youngest, Frances Liberta, survived until 1910 and the age of eighty-one. The life of Frances Liberta is a story in itself. She was conceived during the father's "lodging" in York jail—hence the name Liberta—and was only five years old when orphaned. Maurice Scollard, a clerk in the Bank of Upper Canada, became the children's guardian and administered their estate with great care.

In 1848 Frances Liberta became Sister Saint Maurice of the Congregation of Notre Dame in Montreal, her name in religion being a touching tribute to her guardian. She became Mother Superior of the congregation's Mount Saint Bernard institution in the county of Antigonish, Nova Scotia, and it is recorded that her inheritance was spent "in educating poor children."

The vicissitudes visited on the Collins family in the 1834 cholera epidemic are ample testimony to the struggle for mere existence of Canadian pioneers. John Collins died two weeks before Francis, a victim of the same plague. Ann Moore was herself no stranger to suffering. The following passage from R. Barry O'Brien's *The Life of Lord Russell of Killowen* sets out in stark simplicity one of the horror stories of the 1798 Rebellion in Ulster. The speaker is Sarah Russell, later Mother Emmanuel of the Convent of Mercy, Newry:

> I have heard my mother tell stories of '98. Her father was a captain of a merchant ship; he was drowned at sea. Her mother married a second time—Mr Moore of Belfast. One day, in 1798, she was standing at the door of her house—my mother was then seven years old—with a baby in her arms, when a soldier coming up spoke rudely to her. Mr Moore was standing by. He expostulated with the soldier, whereupon the latter made a lunge of the bayonet at my grandmother, and drove the point through the baby's eye. The child was killed on the spot; then the soldier ran away. Mr Moore followed him to the barracks and told what had happened. But all the satisfaction Mr Moore got was that he was sent to gaol for six weeks.

Thus did Ann Moore know tragedy from earliest childhood.

The Essence of Collins Distilled

On Education
Canadian Freeman, 1 December 1825

Common Schools.—We promised some time ago to lend our humble assistance, so far as our slender talents would permit, in calling the attention of the legislature to the present system of Common Schools in this Province, and we see no object so worthy of their consideration . . . It is said that Common School teachers have already a bounty of £10 a year, which ought to be considered as a sufficient encouragement.—But we deny that it is any thing like an adequate encouragement for a man of talents to settle in the remote parts of the country; and even if it were, it does not operate as a bounty at all, under the present system; because the school signers in general seize upon this sum, (evidently contrary to the intention of the Government, as they cannot draw the money) and deduct it from the salary of the teacher.

We therefore hope that the House will take up this first of all subjects, and give it due consideration.

On Dangerous Drivers
Canadian Freeman, 18 January 1827

The sleighing was never better in this part of the country than it is at present, and Patrick Swift's people [an allusion to W.L. Mackenzie] of quality, in *little* York, lately removed from the water raft and the kitchen, are determined to enjoy it, with a vengeance, by driving over every foot passenger that comes in their way—thus verifying the old age [*sic*] which says:—

"Set a beggar on horseback, and he'll ride to the Devil."

Not long since, a poor decrepit old Scotchman, named Sandy McDougall was trampled down by one of our Bank quill-drivers in a two-horse sleigh, while carrying a bucket of water across the main street of York, and his leg is so lacerated that it is feared amputation will be necessary, in order to save his life.—

Several other accidents have occurred by rapid driving, and on last Sunday, as we were coming from Church, our lives were endangered, and very nearly lost, by the family of a Judge in this town, who drove through a whole congregation, passing men, women, horses, and sleighs, with the utmost indifference as to life or property, at the rate of about ten knots an hour, with a half-bred African at the helm! Is there no law in little York to take hold of Mungo, and the Judge's horses for this outrage? If not we think the Solons of Upper Canada who are assembled in our legislative halls, could not have a better subject to provide for. In the mean time, in order to meet the impudence of Patrick Swift's nobility, with a reasonable degree of resentment, we intend to carry a tolerable piece of hickory, and the first among them, be him judge or magistrate, that refuses to give one side of the King's high way, we shall endeavour to make such application to the head of his horse or driver, according (as may be convenient,) as will secure to us the privilege of a British Subject; and we recommend to all those who have not the convenience of keeping coachmen in livery to resort to this reasonable mode of self-defence, against such intolerable insolence as is experienced in the neighbourhood of York, every hour in the day in this respect, until time be had for legislative interference.

On Union with Lower Canada
Canadian Freeman, 28 August 1828

The question of a *Union* with Lower Canada has been brought before the imperial Parliament by a few speculating London merchants, and brother Carey thinks that three-fourths of our new *radical* members will be in favour of the measure. We have not given this subject due consideration as yet, but our present impression is, that if three-fourths of the new Parliament be in favour of an Union, three-fourths of them will be enemies to the true interests of Upper Canada. We recollect when this question was formerly agitated here, Mr Carey at first supported the measure, but changed his mind afterwards, and opposed it. Perhaps he will now go over the same course. We see a great deal to lose by a Union with Lower Canada—but very little to gain.

On Castlereagh
Canadian Freeman, 4 September 1828

ORIGIN OF THE LONDONDERRY FAMILY
The history of this family is curious, and merits particular notice. The real name is Gregor, the first of whom, who figured in Ireland, was one Rob Gregor, a Scotch pedlar, who had been in the practice of trading to the County Down, in cast clothes; but having in a broil at the fair of Dunbarton, knocked out a man's eye, he fled his country altogether, and became a pack carrier through Ulster, in the service of one Robinson, a shopkeeper in Newtown Ards, with whom, heretofore, he used to do his traffic on his account. After a while Robinson died childless—leaving his shop and a Bishop's lease of a couple score pounds a year value, to his widow, who married Rob. They had a son bred to the father's and mother's business, who grew up, and in process of time, paid his addresses to a girl of Newtown Ards of the name of Orr . . . to whom the youth was attached by a prospect she was said to have from a man of Stewart, her maternal uncle, who had been gone some years to seek his fortune in India, where, report said, he had been successful; and who at length died abroad, and left his niece a considerable property—so much beyond Gregor's anticipation that he even wanted assurance to continue his suit . . . They were married and Gregor thereupon assumed the royal name of Stewart, without license of the Herald's office . . . They had a son Rob, or Robert, who was to be educated as a gentleman, now a great name, and who, in the progress of time, was sent to the Temple to study the law—or rather to eat his way to the bar. Stewart, the father, had purchased two estates with Miss Orr's money, and had gained some footing in

the borough of Newtown Ards. A great man in land, in the county Down, at that time, was the Earl of Hertford, an English nobleman. To him our young Stewart became known, and actually obtained one of his daughters in marriage.—His father dying, he was now a man of property, with great alliance—*owner of a borough* —in fact *one of us*—and at length being raised to the *peerage*, because of so much influence that, in the year 1799, his son Robert was a candidate for the representation of the county Down, on what is humorously called the popular interest; opposed even to the powerful leading of the Marquis of Downshire, to whose servants' hall the grandfather of Robert would have had a difficulty to gain admittance. This son of Lord Londonderry was the famous Castlereagh, or, as he was jocosely called in the county Down, Castlerag, in allusion to the occupation of his grandfather, the dealer in old clothes. His appointment by the late oligarchy to the prominent situation of manager of St Stephen, proves what a very small talent is requisite for the office.—*Captain Rock's suppressed Volume.*

On Insolvent Debtors
Canadian Freeman, 11 December 1828

Insolvent Debtors.—Of all the countries on earth, we believe there is none in which insolvent debtors are so barbarously treated as in Canada—the laws respecting them are a disgrace to British Jurisprudence—sufficient to put humanity to the blush—and call aloud for wholesome amendment. In Canada, an unfortunate man who incurs a debt of a few dollars, without the means of liquidating it, is liable to be incarcerated, at the discretion of a merciless creditor, during his natural life! At home, no ordinary debt, (except a fraud be proved) can deprive a man of his liberty longer than two or three months—in the U. States the term is still shorter, and they are threatening to abolish the practice altogether. At home, for the few weeks they can be confined, debtors have an opportunity of taking air and exercise, with ballcourts, racket courts, &c. to amuse them. In Canada they are cooped up in a filthy apartment, for life, without bed, bedding, victuals, fuel, or any other thing to support nature, save the bare walls that surround them! Is this just? Is it honest? Is it Christian? Can Heathen persecution exceed it? We have at this moment above our heads, *twelve* able-bodied stout men, committed to this gaol for paltry debts, endeavouring to pass away dull time in playing marbles, like children—without even the consoling ray of hope ourselves enjoy, that at a given period, however distant, an end will be put to their sufferings . . . We would suggest the formation of an Insolvent Debtor's Friend Society, throughout the Colony, and the immediate collection of a general fund for this purpose. In the mean time, we hope the humane inhabitants of York will consult for the comfort of the *Freeman*'s brethren of the attic story, in the approaching holidays.

On Attorney General Robinson
Canadian Freeman, 18 December 1828

From the moment you perceived that my labours tended to open the minds of the people, and frustrate your evil machinations, your "native malignancy" led you to become my deadly enemy, and you have ever since thirsted after my ruin, as the tyger thirsts for blood. Your first attempt to injure me, was about eight years ago when you went to little Dr Horne, the King's Printer, and prevailed upon him to stop me from reporting the debates, which he did, at your instance, for a few days, and when a majority of members induced the Doctor to continue my services to the end of the session, you wrote a note to Dr Horne telling him, in answer to his enquiry whether he was bound by law to pay me, that he need not do so, unless he so pleased. Upon the strength of this opinion, the little Doctor refused to pay—but I sued him and recovered. Was not this "malignancy"? Your next step was to vilify & abuse me, in the House, as an incompetent reporter, in order to prevent the House from employing me, and to prevent the publication of the debates. Was not this "malignancy"? But in this, too, you failed —the House offered me encouragement for six years—the debates were regularly published—the country saw your parliamentary conduct, and marked it with reprobation. You saw yourself dwindling into insignificance, and what was your next step to put me down and stop reporting? You let me go through the business of a whole session—received my newspapers weekly yourself, as well as all the other members, and after making such use of my labours as you saw fit for three months, you then advised Sir Peregrine not to issue his warrant for the payment of my wages, £113 10s. voted by the House, on the vague pretence that the contingent expenses of the House were increasing too rapidly! although you knew well there was no item for which the people who provided the means would so willingly contribute. Was not this "malignancy"? . . .

Finding that I had too much system and economy to be crushed by the loss of £113 10s. you next showed your "native malignancy" by attempting to overwhelm me with libel prosecutions, and at the last Spring Assizes you showered four of them on my head in two days!—What has become of them? Three of them you dared not bring to issue, and on the fourth I was honorably acquitted! Here the country was put to the expense of four frivolous libel indictments at one Assizes, by you, without a single conviction!—And why? Merely to see if you could worry the *Freeman* to beggary or to silence. Is not this "malignancy" of the most noxious character? Is it not bitter, vindictive, and cruel persecution? Is it not an unjustifiable waste of public money? Is it not an intolerable abuse of office, for the purpose of gratifying feelings of private malice?

On the "Miniature Castlereagh"
Canadian Freeman, 25 December 1828

York Gaol, December 25
THE FREEMAN TO MR ATTORNEY
GENERAL ROBINSON
Nam sine vities nemo nascatur,
Optimus ille est que minimus urgetur.—Horace.

There is no man without "native malignancy," and that man is the best to whom the least can be charged.—*Freeman.*

Sir,

In my letter of last week, I confined myself chiefly to your individual "malignancy" towards myself. I shall now proceed to show what I view as "malignancy" towards others—amounting, as I think, on the whole to Judge Sherwood's *learned* improvement on Dr Johnson's definition—"an inclination to injure others!" I have viewed you, Sir, as a Castlereagh in miniature. Castlereagh was a man of extraordinary talents, of tolerable private character, at the same time the corruptest minister that ever disgraced the British Cabinet—a man that in private life had some regard for principle, while as a political man he was bound by no tie, and sacrificed every thing to the will of his employer, in order to gratify his own boundless ambition. You, Sir, seem to me to be directly of the Castlereagh *genus* of politicians, bearing the same proportion of power and ability, when compared to your great prototype, that a *cat* does to a *tyger*!

On Banking
Canadian Freeman, 1 January 1829

Fire Insurance Company.—As Little York is beginning to burst her swaddling-clothes, the establishment of a Fire Insurance Company is talked of. We approve very much of the idea and hope it will speedily be carried into effect.—But as the York Bank [Collins is referring to the Bank of Upper Canada] has been turned into a political scourge upon the people, we think their first exertions ought to be to check its influence by some means or other, and it appears to us this could most effectually be done by the establishment of another Bank in this town upon liberal principles. What secured the Attorney General's return to Parliament last election? The York Bank—and after the election closed, the Institution, we hear, stooped to the grossest partiality in throwing out the paper of some of the safest and best men, who voted against the Attorney General, while it opened its discounts to others, that voted for the Attorney, who were comparatively men of straw! This, we believe, is known to every man in York, and so long as *two black-balls* have this power, and that the Attorney General himself and his dear brother-in-law, D'Arcy Boulton (*honest* D'Arcy) have the command of them, the thing is easily accounted for. We had in our hands, the other day, a bill for £250, backed by six or eight of the most wealthy and respectable mercantile men in the Districts of Gore and Niagara, which was black-balled in the York Bank, merely, as we believe, because some two or three of the Directors have long wished to crush the person in whose favour it was drawn. Is this much longer to be endured? We think not. We therefore advise the people first to establish a Bank upon liberal principles, and then to get up Fire Insurance and other Companies, as the increase of population and the exigencies of the times may require.

(In June of the same year, Collins had his wish met:)

Canadian Freeman, 25 June 1829

New Bank.—We are happy to find that a branch of the Montreal Bank has commenced operations in this town, and hope it will finally extinguish the Bank of Upper Canada, which, from its political bias, and illiberal character, is viewed by many as a curse, instead of a blessing in the country.

On Constitutional Reform
Canadian Freeman, 25 June 1829

The fact is now undeniable, that ministers at home are determined to uphold the corrupt faction that have so long oppressed the colony—who will now become fearless in their villany. What then is to be done by the people? We see but one course to save the colony from impending revolution and the horrors of civil war—namely, the immediate formation of a Constitutional Society ... after the manner of the Catholic Association, as we before recommended, and to co-operate with the patriots of Lower Canada in the good work of putting down colonial official corruption and misrule and establishing, on a firm basis, the rights & privileges of the people.

On the Discharge of Firearms
Canadian Freeman, 15 July 1830

Shooting in the Streets.—The streets of this town yesterday, re-
sembled a field of battle by the noise of constant firing at pigeons, in
every direction. We never witnessed such a scene in any civilized
community. The shot fell like hail on the heads of passengers, and
roofs of houses, and it was at the risk of life and limb that any person
went out. A person would imagine there was not a police officer in
town! We are happy to hear, however, that when our sleeping
policemen awoke, about 4 o'clock in the afternoon, some of the
delinquents were recognized and fined, so that we hope a trifling
check will be given to so gross a violation of law and decency.

On Ideal Parliamentarians
Canadian Freeman, 23 October 1830

We want no parties in our Assembly, neither ministerial nor popular—we want no political mountebanks, to waste the public time
in empty gaggling—we want steady, honest men who will put
their shoulders to the wheel and endeavour to develop the resources of the country, going hand in hand with the Executive,
when right, and checking it coolly, when wrong. This was our
opinion from the first—and accordingly, when the old "Reptile
Band," under Sir P. Maitland, were driving their despotic sway in
the Assembly, we resisted them fearlessly, and aided by the Press
and public opinion, we may say we put them down—although
forty-five weeks' close confinement in York Castle was our
reward...

On Charity
Canadian Freeman, 25 November 1830

Having spent part of our early life in Dublin, and frequently acted
as a collector, upon such occasions, in some of the churches, we
have seen poor looking men and women, without even the appearance of comfort in their dress, cheerfully throwing on the plate

of charity several pieces of silver each week, and knowing that this
was customary with them, almost every Sunday, and given too out
of the miserable weekly pittance which a mechanic's labour there
affords, it made an impression upon our mind that can never be
obliterated. We therefore hope, that as the calls of charity are few
in this country, they will be promptly and liberally attended to,
and that the clergy, on calling upon their flocks, once in the quarter
or half year, in future, instead of apologizing to them for doing it *so
often*, will congratulate them that it is so seldom the poor of this
place require a helping hand.

On Roads, Railways, and Canals
Canadian Freeman, 23 December 1830

The awful state of the roads, for some weeks past, and the very
laudable solicitude of His Excellency Sir John Colborne for an
improvement in the present road system, have turned the attention
of everyone to this important subject, and all eyes are fixed upon
our new House of Assembly to see what plan they will adopt for
taking us out of the mud. At this crisis, then, when the Legislature is
about to meet, we think it behoves every man who has the interest
of the Province at heart, and who is capable of expressing an idea
upon the subject, to come forward with whatever information he
may possess. We approve of His Excellency's suggestion respecting
the commutation of statute-labour—for we think that one shilling
from each man put into the hands of a skilful contractor, would do
more than half a dollar in the present way. But as to toll-gates, we
are wholly opposed to them. We think the King's highway ought to
be free to all... It seems to us that nature intended that the chief
communication in this Province should be by water, and while
lavish in her gifts in this way, she has denied good materials for
roads.—Therefore, instead of throwing away the public funds in
casting mud upon mud, every Spring, on Yonge-street, we should
at once set about the cutting of a canal from Lake Simcoe to
York... Is it not disgraceful to us that the very wood we burn in
York is brought from the United States, when the cutting of twenty
or thirty miles of canal would open to York and the country at large

such a mine of wealth?... Some people are very anxious for railways, like our correspondent of last week. Now we do not view railways as at all suited to the common business of this country, where oxen and horses follow each other on the highway in mingled succession—and as to laying a wooden railway, it is all nonsense—the material is too perishable. An iron railway in such a section as that from Queenston to Chippewa, might do well for steam carriages—but in our opinion, when a railway is contemplated at all, it must be for one description of power, be that steam, horse, or ox...

On Corruption
Canadian Freeman, 9 December 1830

A Peep into the Clerk's Office, House of Assembly.—After considerable inquiry respecting this office, we are led to believe that greater extravagance and more gross corruption has been carried on in it, during the short reign of the *saddlebags* faction, than any other department or office under the government of this Province, and as we have now a House of Assembly composed of men a majority of whom are independent of that hypocritical and knavish party, we think it our duty to bring this matter under their serious consideration. In touching this subject, we do not mean to insinuate that Col. Fitzgibbon, the Clerk of the House, has been the chief actor, or that he had anything to do with it more than by connivance and crouching servility to that party while in power—no, *Saint* Patrick, his deputy, seems to have had the sole control of the Clerk's office, for the last two years, and the game appears to have been carried on between him and certain members of the late house... He dictates to poor Fitzgibbon (who has latterly been a mere cypher in his hands) as to the employment of clerks, and if a Ryersonian ranter like Vaux can be had, no other man has the least chance of employment. We do not know whether the *Saint* has a per centage on those situations—but we know that a man who is taken in to earn £6 a day, can well afford a handsome *douceur*, and we know a certain class of hypocrites who never refuse a kindness of that sort... This is *saintly* work—will the present House tolerate it? We hope not—we trust the first motion will be to appoint a committee to inquire into the corruption of the Clerk's office, and that the authors of fraud and injustice, if any such be connected with it, will be brought to condign punishment...We think that a more competent man than Patrick can be had to fill his place at members' wages, £2 a day, and that £10 a week would be a fair remuneration for the other gentlemen of the *quill*, as other wages now go. We see a number of young men, and excellent clerks too, hunting for situations, who would gladly accept such pay. We shall refresh the memory of the House, upon this subject, as soon as the session opens.

On Vaccination
Canadian Freeman, 26 May 1831

Vaccination.—We are requested to state that a medical gentleman will attend daily at the Hospital in this town, to vaccinate *gratis* the children of the poor, and that a quantity of matter for that purpose is now on hands. We advise them to embrace this favourable opportunity lest the arrival of emigrant families introduce so terrible a malady, and spread sickness and death amongst their children.

On Whore Houses
Canadian Freeman, 26 May 1831

> *And the Lord rained upon Sodom and Gomorrah brimstone and fire from the Lord out of heaven. And he destroyed these cities, and all the country about, all the inhabitants of the cities, and all things that spring from the earth.*—Gen.

We witnessed such scenes last week as induced us to think that more shameless and barefaced debauchery was never exhibited in Sodom and Ghomorrha, than is carried on in this town at present. Houses of infamy are scattered thro' every corner of the town— and one of them had the hardihood to commence operations next door to our office, last week, in a house under the control of a Police magistrate! Although this house was kept by a degraded negro family, so besotted are some of our would-be young gentlemen —

so lost to shame and decency—and so dead to every feeling of Christianity—that they crowded to it at noon-day, and some of them that we know visited it in open day, last Sabbath!—Young lawyers, and others of respectable standing. We had no idea before that such wretched and shameless depravity existed in our infant community—in any other place that we have lived, such men would be viewed as a walking pestilence and scouted out of all decent society. It seems to to us that some of our authorities, and heads of families too, connive at debauchery of this kind, which, if not checked, will be sufficient ere long to draw down the wrath of God upon the town, as in times of old upon Sodom and Gomorrha. By some trouble and loss of time, we got our new neighbours ejected on Monday last—the Police are acquainted with the parties, and if they do not do their duty, we shall try the Executive.

On Religious Bigotry and "the Glorious Twelfth"
Canadian Freeman, 23 June 1831

This, thank God, is a land of civil and religious liberty, where every man enjoys the freedom of conscience, and every Irishman whose blood has been cooled by one or two Canadian winters must see the blind folly of party spirit and religious animosity, so long the scourge and degradation of his native land.—A day then is approaching (the 12th July) which has not passed by, in Ireland, for many years, without riot and bloodshed. In this Province, too, some of our pious countrymen have attempted to butcher each other, *for the sake of religion*, at Kingston and elsewhere, on the memorable day of *Christian benevolence*, to the great edification of other Christians from all quarters of the globe. But we call upon every Irishman . . . Orangeman or Catholic, who respects his own character and that of his country, to aid and assist in putting down such folly as party processions, party quarrels, and religious animosity, which have long been the bane and ruin of our native land, and the reproach of Irishmen all over the world.

On Water Pollution
Canadian Freeman, 5 April 1832

York Bay. It is really astonishing how the magistrates can allow the horrible nuisance which now appears on the face of this Bay. All the filth of the town—dead horses, dogs, cats, manure, &c. heaped up together on the ice, to drop down, in a few days, into the water which is used by almost all the inhabitants on the Bay shore. If they have no regard for the health of their fellow-beings, are they not afraid to poison the fish that supply their own tables? We hope that His Excellency will take cognizance of the state of the Bay from the Garrison down, and see the carrion-broth to which the worshipful magistracy are about to treat the inhabitants when the ice dissolves. There is not a drop of good well-water about the Market-square, and the people are obliged to use the Bay water however rotten.—Instead therefore of corrupting the present bad supply, we think the authorities ought rather adopt measures to supply the town from the pure fountain that springs from the Spadina and Davenport Hill, which could be done at a trifling expense. There is nothing more conducive to health than good water—nothing more destructive than bad—and what ought the authorities to watch over and protect before the health of the community?

On the Circus
Canadian Freeman, 31 October 1833

THE CIRCUS

We visited the Circus last evening for the first time, and felt pleasure in seeing it fitted up in a superior manner. A *new pony* Selin went thro' his duty admirably, and showed what can be done by that noble animal, the Horse, when well tried.—Mr Jackson performed on the slack rope, and seems much improved since we saw him perform before. Mr Sweet then came out on the tight rope, and under the disadvantage of performing upon a rope not sufficiently braced he showed inimitable performance. As a horseman and a tumbler he is also far superior to any performer who has visited this place, and is highly worthy of public patronage.

Mr M'Cleary has been engaged for a few nights, and his benefit will take place on Saturday next, when the greatest novelty ever produced here will be brought forward. On this occasion, Mr M'Cleary will give a variety of entertainments, with an entire new Song called "The English Irish Scotchman," which was received in London for upwards of fifty nights with the greatest applause. Mr M'Cleary's abilities as a singer & comic actor are too well known in this place to require further recommendations from us, and we have only to hope that he will meet with that liberal patronage which his merits deserve, and which has been uniformly bestowed upon them by the inhabitants of York.

On the Cholera
Canadian Freeman, 24 July 1834

The Cholera.—It appears by private accounts from Montreal and Quebec, that this awful malady has again visited those cities, with all the malignity of 1832—but the newspapers received yesterday from those places are silent on the subject.

The *Freeman* for 24 July 1834 is the last issue to survive. On 28 August Collins died of cholera.

> *Where the crown of hope is nearest,*
> *Where the voice of joy is clearest,*
> *Where the heart of youth is lightest,*
> *Where the light of love is brightest,*
> *There is death.*

John Ruskin, "The Broken Chain"
(written in 1839)

Hansard: Its Function and Its Worth

Verba volant, scripta manent.
(Spoken words fly away, written words remain).

T O write down, and to print and publish the spoken words
of Canada's parliamentarians is the function of *Hansard*
in the Parliament of Canada.

Let the reader think what he will of Parliament. "We are all
ashamed of it," wrote Robert Louis Stevenson. "Talk of mobs!"
exclaimed Hazlitt. "Show me the House of Commons. It is like
Smithfield on a market day or a cockpit in all its glory." Charles
Dickens always referred to it as "the great dust heap of Westminster."

Edward Allen Talbot was no less harsh on Canadian legislators,
whom he described as "a motley crew."

> If a shop-keeper, who gives liberal credit, appears on the hustings,
> he is sure to be elected; but if no such person presents himself, the
> freeholders invariably select the greatest fool in the lot, consoling
> themselves with the idea that, though he may do but little good, he
> can do no harm.*

Stevenson, Hazlitt, Dickens, and Talbot lived in an era when
parliamentary democracy was struggling to escape from the
confining grasp of the owners of rotten boroughs and, in Canada, of
the Family Compact. Escape it did, and in large measure it was
because of the efforts of pioneer *Hansard* reporters and publishers.

In an address to the Ottawa Arts and Letters Club in 1928,

---

*In *Five Years' Residence in the Canadas*, op. cit., Vol. I, p. 403.

Martin Burrell, parliamentary librarian, and himself a former parliamentarian and minister of state, asked:

> Who or what is Hansard? I venture to present this Canadian inheritor of a great name and a great tradition as an Author-Compiler-Editor unique in his class. He has given us a literature more voluminous, more important, and, in many respects, not less fascinating than the output of all his brethren of the craft ... In these innumerable tomes are reflected the struggles, the aspirations, the futilities, the wisdom, and the achievements of a nation. Here lies the record of the evolution of our widening liberties and the story of the long road of progress. ...
>
> Hansard exists, not for the legislator alone but, in a real sense, for the nation. If the theory of democracy is sound and is to endure; if the people do really govern, then it is worth much to them to know that they have access to everything that has transpired in their own Parliament.

If *Hansard* had not written down the spoken words of Canada's legislators, those words would long since have been lost. This happened with Canada's first experiments in parliamentary representation, and the shortsightedness has been decried ever since.

Sir John A. Macdonald, first Prime Minister of a united Canada, was among those to deplore the absence of such a printed record. Even today, researchers and historians are painstakingly attempting to create or structure, from fragmented newspaper accounts and other sources, a *Hansard* for the years from 1840 until the appearance of an official publication forty years later.* Burrell quoted Lord Balfour with telling effect on this point:

> The only form of history which is really immortal is the contemporary record from which future historians draw their materials. Every generation will insist on rewriting the history of the past in its own fashion. But the original sources remain. They only remain; they only are perpetual.†

*Since 1970 a total of seventeen volumes of the *Debates of the Legislative Assembly of United Canada* have been produced, using such sources.

†Martin Burrell, *Betwixt Heaven and Charing Cross* (Toronto: The Macmillan Company of Canada Limited, 1928), pp. 263, 276.

In short, *Hansard* is the legislative history of the country, recorded in the making. The *Hansard* reporter, sitting at a desk, right in the centre of the House of Commons, has "an inner-ring seat to history in the making." Yet this was not always the case.

For centuries the Westminster "Mother of Parliaments" (a popular misnomer) jealously guarded the deliberations of its members from appearance in print. That there was good reason for such a precaution in earlier times cannot be gainsaid. Members could be exposed to retaliation if their speeches were ill-received by the Crown. But, with the lessening of the role of the monarchy, that reason became of more and more doubtful validity, although the precaution itself continued to be taken.

The new newspapers and magazines that made their appearance in the 1700s were rebuffed in their attempts to report Parliament. Any reporter in the Public Gallery who tried to take notes of members' speeches was liable to arrest and imprisonment. A trace of this practice lingers to the present day in a number of legislatures which forbid visiting members of the public to take notes while listening to the speeches of their representatives.

When barred from writing shorthand, some reporters relied solely on their recollections of members' speeches, later writing out longhand reports for their newspapers. Their ability to do so is preserved in the names of "Memory Woodfall" in London and "Memory Martin" in Dublin, whose feats of memorised reporting have since become legendary. Having listened to an entire day's or evening's debate, each uncannily could dictate up to sixteen newspaper columns of correct reportage.

Almost all recent accounts of the part played by Samuel Johnson (the lexicographer whose dictionary was denied to the jury in the trial of Francis Collins) in the reporting of parliamentary debates have mightily smitten him hip and thigh for allegedly colouring his reports from 1740 to 1743. Johnson, it is true, based his reports on notes supplied by others, including the historian Guthrie, and did not himself frequent the House of Commons. Yet, despite the much quoted remark, first attributed to him by Sir John Hawkins, that he took care "to give the Whig dogs the worst of it," more than sixty years later William Cobbett, in good conscience, was able to come to the defence of the besmirched reputation of the good Dr Johnson. The following quotation may help restore some balance to current perspective on the matter:

> The story... is disbelieved by Cobbett, who by comparing Johnson's reports with Archbishop Secker's manuscript Diary, is able to bear testimony to their general fidelity.*

Not all Members of Parliament in Westminster were opposed to their speeches being taken down and published. A noteworthy exception was Sir Henry Cavendish who, as a sitting member from 1768 to 1774, took down in shorthand those debates which he adjudged the most important in the life of the thirteenth Parliament, otherwise known as "The Unreported Parliament." Cavendish gave some of the background to his surreptitious note-taking when he wrote that he was unable "to take some speeches because the disorder which prevailed, the premature applause, and the favourite words 'Hear, hear', so frequently echoed through the House, forbade a hearing." The *Hansard* reporter of two hundred years later, on reading Cavendish, might well say, "Plus ça change, plus c'est la même chose."

In 1881 Sir John A. Macdonald mentioned Cavendish's efforts when he repelled an attempt to have the infant *Hansard* reporting service in Canada's Parliament discontinued. Indeed, Canadian historians are greatly indebted to Cavendish for his reporting of the debates on The Quebec Act, passed on 22 June 1774.

In a work detailing some of the history of *Hansard* in Canada's fully bilingual Parliament, it is worth recounting that, in contrast to the situation at Westminster, the National Assembly of France from its inception showed a great willingness and determination to provide assistance for the reporting of its debates. Again to quote Balch's *Universal Cyclopaedia:*

> They managed things better in France, for only four years later (1787) the French Assembly voted that Maret—afterwards well known as the Duc de Bassano—then engaged in reporting the

---

Ready Reference (The Universal Cyclopaedia) compiled by William Ralston Balch, and published by Griffith Farran Browne & Co., Ltd., 35 Bow St., London, 1889.

debates for the *Bulletin de l'Assemblée*, should have a special seat allotted to him. Though it was the fashion to extol England as a model in things Parliamentary, the Assembly did not imitate this peculiarity of the British Parliament, for every facility was given to make the public acquainted with the debates. Barrère's reports in the daily journal *Point du Jour*, had a great circulation; and Lehodey organised a regular corps whose reports appeared in the *Journal des Etats Généraux*, the title of which was afterwards changed into the *Journal Logographique*.

Not until sixteen years later did *Cobbett's Parliamentary Debates* make its appearance in London.

An Official and Permanent *Hansard*

T HE jargon is peculiarly parliamentary, but its presen-
tation to the House of Commons of Canada on Mon-
day, 26 April 1880 represented the culmination of sixty years of
struggle to establish an official and permanent *Hansard.*

Your Committee begs leave to submit the following Resolution: —
Resolved, That as greater permanency in the *personel* [*sic*] of the
Reporting Staff would ensure a higher degree of efficiency, the
Committee would recommend that six Reporters be engaged and
recognized as Officers of the House, subject to such regulations
as may from time to time be enacted by the Commissioners for the
Internal Economy of the House, or by the Select Committee ap-
pointed to supervise the Official Report of the Debates of the House.

This was the third report of the select committee appointed to
supervise the reporting of the debates. Two days later the report
was adopted by the House. The following quotation from the
debate of 28 April 1880 sums up the intent of the legislators for all
time and the purpose of the new *Hansard.* The speaker is Mr Ross,
MP for West Middlesex:

One of the greatest faults of the old contract system was that the
contractor having a lump sum for the reporting, a special inducement was held out to him to secure cheap men, or pay a low rate for
the reporting. Consequently, it sometimes happened that the staff
was not composed of the best men to be found in that profession.
Under the new system we have fixed the minimum salary at $1,000,
and a salary of $1,500 for the chief, believing that at these figures we
can get the best talent and the most experienced stenographers in
the country. Their being officers of the House will give dignity as

140

Edward J. Quirk

well as permanency to their employment, which will dispose these gentlemen to make it their ambition to qualify themselves as thoroughly as possible for their work, to remain a number of years in the service, and by their experience, if by no other means, secure that efficiency which will qualify them for the discharge of their duty well...I believe a staff of six will be able to give us a full enough report of our Debates, will secure us more accurate reports than we have already yet secured, and make the Official Reports of the debates more satisfactory and more reliable than they have been under the old system.

Six days later, Mr Stephenson of the select committee presented its fourth report, stating that the following selection was made: "Mr *Bradley*, as Chief Reporter. Messrs. *Abbott, Duggan, Horton, Eyvil* [*sic*], and *Watson* as Assistants." It also recommended that Mr J.C. Boyce be engaged to assist in the Reporting Room. This was on 4 May, recognized ever since as *Hansard*'s birthday, although formal adoption of the report did not take place until two days later.

Mr Ross's belief in the inducement "to remain a number of years in the service, and by their experience, if by no other means, secure that efficiency which will qualify them for the discharge of their duty well" has been borne out over the years, and nowhere is better exemplified than in the person of Mr Eddie Quirk, successor to the aforementioned Boyce. Mr Quirk, son of the late Dr Edward L. Quirk, of Aylmer, Quebec, first joined the House of Commons staff in 1928 and has given a lifetime of service to *Hansard*. It has been said truthfully that he is a man who has more intimate knowledge of *Hansard*, of what makes it tick, of the reasons why, and the precedents for, than any other on Parliament Hill. "Ask Eddie Quirk"; when everything else fails, but more often before anything else is tried, that phrase is heard, in *Hansard* and far beyond the confines of *Hansard*.

Despite the adoption of the select committee's third and fourth reports, there was still a body of opinion that held that the reporting of parliamentary debates was wrong and that there was no worth "in handing them down to posterity." In the eleventh month of the new *Hansard*'s existence, a motion was moved by Mr MacDonnell, MP for Inverness, that called for the discontinuance of the official reporting and publication of speeches. It was a last echo of the old Family Compact argument, one which had served its purpose well in the days of John Carey and Francis Collins, and which had sufficient force left in 1867 to prevent the establishment of an official *Hansard*. But the passage of time had exposed it for what it was, a desire to maintain a barrier between elected representative and elector. It was the old argument against freedom of information. Swift's

> *Let them, when they once get in*
> *Sell the Nation for a Pin;*

and sell it unreported, was the nub of the matter.

Twenty-three years had passed since Macdonald and Cartier had unsuccessfully fought for a *Hansard*. This was now Sir John A. Macdonald, Prime Minister of Canada, speaking, and he threw the full weight of his official and personal prestige into the fight to save an independent parliamentary report. His speech occupied less than a full page, but here was the greatest parliamentarian of his generation presenting *Hansard* with its charter and freedom from interference:

Then we are driven to the original resolution to do away with the Hansard altogether. As I said before, that rests with the House. But I think it would be a retrograde step, it would be unjust to the great body of the House. If we can afford it—and we can afford it—every hon. member who represents a constituency has a right to have his speech reported; for we are all equal here, we are all equally interested and have equal rights and responsibilities; we all have the same rights; the youngest member has the same right as the oldest member, to have his utterances as fully spread out in the official report as the leader of the House or of the Opposition. It would be a retrograde step, it would be a mistake, it would be a historical blunder. We all know the regrets that are expressed by every literary man, every political man, every statesman, and every historian, that the speeches made by the great men in the days of old were, in consequence of the practice of Parliament, lost forever. I think it was the younger Pitt who said that he would rather have a lost speech of Lord Bolingbroke than all the lost pages of Livy. We have no speeches of Chatham; no speeches of Bolingbroke; none of the great speeches made in the Long Parliament, at the time of the fight between freedom and tyranny, in the time of Charles I. We all know how eagerly historians have looked up every little sentence which can be discovered, any casual note taken, any remark made by any of the leaders of public opinion from the time of Queen Elizabeth until now. If you open a history and read about those days you will find how imperfect are the notes of Cavendish, the mere scraps preserved by Strange, or Gray, or by any others who took notes of public utterances of the statesmen of those times, and yet how eagerly they are scanned in order that historians may find out the motives that moved the body of Parliament—not merely the leaders of Parliament, but the great mass of parliamentarians, because it is the general opinion of Parliament, and not the opinion of the leaders of the day that shows what the public pulse is. It is the expression of opinion by the mass of the members that shows really what the feelings of the people are as expressed by their representatives. Even in Canada how deeply interesting would be a Hansard showing the debates in the old Province of Upper Canada, or of Lower Canada, giving the discussions in 1791 and 1792 when the two Legislatures were formed. If we had that, it would be the most interesting volume in the world, and every Canadian would read with the deepest interest the speeches on the subjects that engaged the attention of the members of Parliament of those days. He would learn what the chief subject of interest of the people, what the style of speaking and the manner of thought, not of one or two great leaders, but the great body of the representatives of the people, were in those early days. And we are in a great measure without a colonial history. We have no means of tracing out the very groundwork of all our legislation—the motives and impulses of those petty municipal questions which were the chief subjects of interest in the early days, and which have expanded into the larger subjects which are now engaging the attention of the people and the Legislature of Canada. As a matter of history, it is of the very greatest importance that the remarks of every hon. member, who has a responsibility as the representative of the people should, if we can afford it—and we can afford it—be as fully recorded in the official report as those of a leader. I hope we shall not commit such a great mistake, I hope we shall not make such a relapse into barbarism as to throw over the only means by which after generations shall be able to learn what were the subjects of interest engaging our attention, what was the style of speaking and the style of thought, and what were the moving impulses of the people and their representatives in Parliament.*

It need scarcely be added that the resolution was defeated, and *Hansard* lived.

*Debates, 7 March 1881, p. 1250.

People and Personages

THE original members of the *Hansard* staff, in the main, were men of newspaper experience, and for many years the Parliamentary Press Gallery supplied new recruits to the staff almost as a matter of course. During that period, newspaper-men used shorthand as one of the tools of the trade, but in later times two events took place which led to a lessening of dependence on the ability to write shorthand. One was the advent of inter-pretative reporting, emphasizing not so much the precise words spoken by a parliamentarian as the meaning and effect of the words. Only brief snatches of verbatim reporting were included in newspaper columns to glue together a reporter's own interpreta-tions. However, there was at least one blessing: the verbatim extracts were usually the same in all newspapers, courtesy of *Hansard*.

Anyone with an interest in the subject can see today's inter-pretative reporting carried to the ultimate on national television newscasts. In the background a Member of Parliament is shown addressing the House. His gestures and the movement of his lips can be seen. In the foreground is the television commentator telling viewers, *in his words*, what the MP is saying, seen but unheard, in the background. It is something practised by all networks. Through a process of *reductio ad absurdum*, to get a balanced inter-pretation, a variety of commentators should be shown in the back-ground, soundless lips in motion, while in the foreground a com-mentators' commentator tells viewers his opinion of their opinions of the opinions expressed by the now completely invisible Member of Parliament.

The second event that led to the reduced need for reporters to use shorthand was the fact that *Hansard* supplied the Press Gallery

House of Commons Official Reporters in 1886. Front Row: E. Joseph Duggan, J.O. Marceau, George B. Bradley (Chief Reporter), Albert Horton, J.C. Boyce   Back Row: George Eyvel, Thomas John Richardson, F.R. Marceau, Stephen A. Abbott.

with its own verbatim copy, on the hour, every hour; hence, the Gallery's need to rely on its own shorthand reporters diminished. Shorthand was no longer an essential tool, and *Hansard* had to turn to the court-reporting fraternity for its staff. When this failed, reporters were recruited from abroad. Indeed, as recently as 1970, six of the nine English *Hansard* reporters were immigrants, and at the time of writing only two of the staff are former newspapermen.

But for the work of two men, Campbell and Bengough, much of the early history of Canada's *Hansard* would be lost. Alexander Colin Campbell, born in Shannonville, Ontario, on 26 September 1857, was the son of William Stewart Campbell and Margaret Brough, both immigrant Scots. He was educated in Montreal and Toronto, and his first job was in an insurance office supervised by his father. Not finding insurance congenial, he next became a printer's apprentice in the office of Hunter, Rose & Company. In his own crisp style, he outlined his subsequent career:

> Offered and accepted a position as local reporter on the Montreal *Gazette*, in the Spring of 1878. Served through the Orange and Green troubles of that year. In the Autumn brought into practice shorthand in reporting speeches by Thomas White, Editor of the *Gazette*, and others. Removed to Toronto as shorthand reporter on *The Globe*, before the close of 1878. Junior member of *Globe* parliamentary staff 1880, afterwards in charge of *Globe* House of Commons report until 1891. Shorthand work for a Senate committee in the session of '91. Reporter for Toronto *Mail and Empire* 1892 and 1893, and in the latter year served on *Hansard* as special reporter to replace T. J. Richardson, who had broken his arm in a fall. On death of Mr Richardson was appointed in his place in 1894, by resolution of the House confirming report of the Committee on Debates. Being next in seniority ranks, was appointed Associate Editor in 1917 on retirement of Mr Albert Horton to the Editorship of Senate Debates, and the promotion of Thomas P. Owens to the Editorship of *Hansard*. On the death of Mr Owens in 1921 was appointed Editor. Retired effective January 1, 1926. Wishes to be remembered as one who (1) tried to keep in mind always that *Hansard* is not only an immediate service to the House and the country but is also the

greatest single mass of historical material in Dominion affairs; (2) promoted steadily the keeping of the Daily Index; (3) restored the page headings of the Revised Edition; (4) favoured the re-arrangement of the *Hansard* offices which provides a rest room for the women of the staff.*

On 23 April 1932, then nearly seventy-five, A. C. Campbell delivered an address to a meeting of the Chartered Stenographic Reporters Association of Ontario, in the Parliamentary Restaurant, in which he gave an account of men and events connected with *Hansard*, without which much of the story would have long since disappeared.

Campbell told the story of many individuals, and among those to whom he paid tribute was Thomas Bengough, who, then in his seventy-ninth year, was still "an active member of the Senate reporting staff and is a most remarkable instance of youth in age."

Thomas Bengough was indeed a remarkable fellow. Born in 1853, he lived a span of ninety-two years until his death at Toronto on 4 January 1945. Five months before Campbell had addressed the stenographers in 1932, Bengough had delivered a paper before a meeting of the same Association at Toronto.

Bengough was a Pitman writer. At the age of twenty-one he had taken on his first reporting assignment:

Early in 1874, two years before the inauguration of the reporting system at present in vogue in Ontario, I attended at Osgoode Hall, Toronto, to report a case that was being tried in the Court of Chancery. For this I received an attendance fee of eight dollars per day.†

Bengough was also a newspaperman but his life-long interest was shorthand. In 1877 he became an official court reporter, and from 1881 to 1889 published *The Cosmopolitan Shorthander*, a magazine devoted to disseminating knowledge about shorthand. He also

---

*An autobiographical note on the back of a photograph in *Hansard* office.

†From an address to the Chartered Stenographic Reporters Association of Ontario (CSRA) at Toronto, 21 November 1931.

found time to run a business college, and to become a representative of the Remington Typewriter Company. In 1910 he left court reporting to become Secretary to the Royal Commission on Technical Education, and in 1911 joined the Senate reporting staff, retiring eventually in 1932. An obituary in *The Chartered Shorthand Reporter* of March 1945 concluded with this eulogy:

> Perhaps his most lasting monument will be the standardization of Pitmanic reporting shorthand, a movement which he initiated in 1908. At the dinner given in Toronto by a number of professional friends in honour of his 90th birthday many high tributes were paid to him and his remarkable and inspiring career; and on that occasion Mr John J. Healy, a Past President of the National Shorthand Reporters Association, said that among American reporters Mr Bengough was known as "the father of standardization." He spent freely of his time and energy in seeking to elevate the reporting profession, and his work in this regard will continue to bear fruit for long years to come.

Thomas Bengough's reminiscences in manuscript form are a precious legacy to both the Ontario legal and court reporting professions, and from them may also be culled much of interest to the legislative story. A casual reference in these memoirs to John Buskard of Brantford, Ontario, being appointed a court reporter in 1912 provides a natural introduction to a brief account of the career of one of the latter's sons.

W. Warren Buskard, Editor of Debates in the House of Commons from 1957 to 1969, was that son. He was born in Brantford on 14 January 1904. An older brother also became a court reporter, and Warren started to learn the rudiments of shorthand in his tenth year. By sixteen he had advanced sufficiently to be able to undertake mundane, regular court reporting tasks, and three years later was successful in a competition to fill a post on the Ottawa parliamentary committee reporting staff, the training ground for future *Hansard* reporters. His forty-seven years of *Hansard* experience, exceeded only by that of Edward Quirk, left an indelible mark on the reporting of the legislative history of his country, and on those who had the honour to serve with him. The professional respect accorded him was unparalleled, and the

Alexander Colin Campbell

standards he set by his own personal example will forever remain difficult to equal.

Testimony to that respect came when he, and his confrère, Edward L. Featherston, were chosen to report the Royal Commission on Espionage, popularly called the Gouzenko Commission. For months they were escorted by members of the Royal Canadian Mounted Police as they reported and transcribed the evidence. Every notebook, scratch-pad, used carbon and piece of wastepaper had to be turned over to the police at the end of each day. Naturally they were under the strictest oath of secrecy. It was a herculean task. Telling testimony to the worth of their service was given by the Hon. Mr Justice Robert Taschereau and the Hon. Mr Justice R. L. Kellock, the commissioners, who, in the "Conclusion" of their report, commented:

> To the Chief Reporters, Mr Featherston and Mr Buskard, their assistants and staffs, we are also grateful. No matter how long or how late the Commission sat the transcript of each day's evidence was available to us next morning. This greatly facilitated our work.

One of Buskard's colleagues, Charles Empringham, reflecting in later years on Buskard's career, had this to say:

> Warren always seemed to get the right pieces in the right places at the right time and, from the standpoint of staff, must be given the highest marks. To him must go full credit for increasing the size of the staff [from 7 to 9 reporters]; for his excellent presentations before Debates Committees that, for years, had been thinking in such picayune terms that he had to shock them into a state of reality; for bringing editorial freedom back to sane and proper limits, and for his courage in taking what were, on frequent occasions, minority positions when dealing with those in authority, when he felt the interests of the staff were in jeopardy.*

The dedication of Warren Buskard is easily recalled in his admonition to each new staff member: "I want you to take *Hansard* home with you every night for a month. I want you to read it from

*From a letter to the author, 9 November 1976.

W. Warren Buskard

beginning to end, daily. I want you to live, breath, sleep, and think *Hansard* for a month." Those who followed his advice never regretted it. During his years in office he halted many attempted inroads on *Hansard*.

Canadians fascinated with the story of Louis Riel may thank Bengough for his reference to the Regina trial. As reported in *Maclean's* magazine on 9 April 1979, every summer since 1967 a play by John Coulter, based on transcripts from the trial, has been performed at Saskatchewan House. He dutifully recalled the appointment of J. S. Monahan to the Ontario court reporting staff in 1881, describing him as having won "fame and shekels as the Official Reporter of the famous trial at Regina of Louis Riel." Little did Bengough, or Monahan, who died as the result of a railway accident while returning from another court assignment, realize that a hundred years later the latter's shorthand report would still be serving a useful purpose.

Notetakers and Notables

T HE first one hundred years of Canada's *Hansard* are notable in many respects, but one of the least remarked upon is the continuity of service of many individuals. From the 1880s to the 1980s only four generations of reporters have been required, from Duggan to Dunbar to Buskard to Fisher. The corpus of experience and knowledge thus handed down has meant that there has always been someone on *Hansard* with personal knowledge of past events and former parliamentarians. Stephen A. Abbott and E. Joseph Duggan, both members of the original 1880 staff, did not retire until 1912. Sir Wilfrid Laurier, speaking on the occasion of their retirement, had this to say:

> I think nobody will object to the superannuation of Mr Abbott and Mr Duggan. They were very good reporters, as everybody knows, and the House will regret that they have been obliged to ask for superannuation, but of course, as with everybody else, the years of service have told upon them, and they feel they are no longer equal to the arduous task of reporting on the floor of this House.

Twenty years later Stephen Abbott was the sole survivor, "a slight but vigorous blue-eyed, full bearded man of 88 years, a bidder for fame a few years ago by the publication of a book of scriptural and prophetic lore under the title *The Pyramids and Israel*."*

One of the original staff, Albert Horton, made a name for himself in both House and Senate annals. His was another shorthand

*A.C. Campbell's address to the CSRA, 23 April 1932.

family. His brother, Edward, was city editor of the Toronto *Globe* before becoming a member of the newly created Ontario court reporting staff. His eldest sister was the first woman typist in Toronto, and, before the typewriter became standard office equipment, she visited Ottawa for several sessions and typed "takes" at her brother's dictation. Later she was to marry Harry J. Emerson and become the mother of H. Horton Emerson, who also became a shorthand writer and joined the Senate reporting staff.

Albert Horton worked as a newspaperman in Toronto and Montreal before being appointed a *Hansard* reporter in 1880. Campbell tells us that "professionally he was a thorough *Hansard* man, the first to realize that *Hansard* must be edited or it must remain forever a mere series of reporters' takes." To him also goes credit for the form of the *Hansard* index, the key to demonstrating the real value of *Hansard* as the record of the legislative history of the country:

> Every plan that will help in causing *Hansard* to be read and understood by the people generally is a benefit to Canada. Everything that facilitates the researches of the historian in this mine of material is a benefit to Canada and to the world.
>
> The form of index is a simple and obvious idea. So is the expansive power of steam, but we honor the memory of James Watt who made the first working mechanism to use that power. Used to the full, this indexing principle makes *Hansard* not a toilers' job but a great living public service.*

Horton succeeded George Bradley as Chief Reporter (the title Editor of Debates was not adopted by the Canadian Parliament until 1912), and in 1916, at an age when most men would have been looking forward to retirement, he did retire, and promptly began a new *Hansard* career. Until that year the Senate debates had been reported under contract by the Holland family. No doubt influenced by the experience of the Commons, the Senate finally decided to set up its own official *Hansard* reporting service, and chose Albert Horton to head it. Horton's move to the Senate drew the following comment from Mr George P. Graham, MP for

*ibid.

South Renfrew: "He is not the first man who has been willing to go from this House to the Senate, and I suppose he will not be the last."*

Before leaving the Horton family story, further reference to his brother Edward must be given, this time from Bengough:

> During the early eighties Mr Horton spent all his spare time and money in the invention and construction of what he called the Typograph—the first visible writing machine in the world. He was able to manufacture a few machines, which were used with great satisfaction by Mr Tyson, myself and others. The machine was exhibited at the Convention of the Canadian Shorthand Society in 1882, and created a fine impression as it possessed the then unique feature of visibility. By reason of the downward thrust of the keys on the paper it was an excellent manifolder. However, due to the difficulties of financing, it never was placed on the market.†

The Horton Typograph was a Canadian invention, forerunner of many that never reached the marketing stage.

One other name listed by Bengough, Nelson R. Butcher, though he was not a *Hansard* man, has a connection with parliamentary reporting. For many years he supplied freelance reporters to the Commons committee staff. Bengough quotes Butcher describing his introduction to the compression of writing:

> I picked up shorthand on a farm. Told the farmer I was studying shorthand, and he said, "Give it up, you have no education for that business. Take a job as a blacksmith's helper." I stuck at the shorthand, and I have been at it ever since, having put up my shingle in 1879.

There are echoes of Talbot and of Cobbett in the above quotation which prompt reference to another man honoured for his service to

*Debates, 17 May 1916, p. 4127.

†T. Bengough in an address to the CSRA, 21 November 1931.

Hansard and the Parliament of Canada: Charles Leslie Empringham, one of the most beloved of *Hansard* editors.

Charles Empringham's recollections of his over thirty years'
service are a storehouse waiting to be opened to a wider public than
the shorthand fraternity. His keen observations of men and events,
from the reporters' desk on the floor of the House of Commons,
shed much light on the speaking habits and idiosyncrasies of four
decades of parliamentarians. From his mind's eye picture of the
stubs of pencils preferred by William Lyon Mackenzie King, to his
word profiles of lesser men of the era, there is much to be learned.
His country has reason to be grateful that Charlie Empringham,
whose father was a farrier, "stuck at the shorthand" like Nelson
Butcher and was not content to apprentice as a blacksmith's
helper. His insistence on preserving the flavour of the speaker has
stood *Hansard* in good stead on many occasions. As he put it himself: "One should be able to read Diefenbaker and recognize it as
the real, vintage emanation—and not a restructured hodge-podge
of some mythical Solon."

Mention of the Right Honourable member for Prince Albert
can never be made without an accompanying anecdote, this time
from a *Hansard* reporter's point of view, and on an occasion of some
moment. This was in May 1966, when an attempt was made by a
person of deranged mind, Paul Joseph Chartier, to "give parliament a blast," by tossing a dynamite bomb from the Ladies Gallery
onto the floor of the Chamber. Providentially, the fuse was mis-
timed and Chartier blew himself to pieces in the washroom on
the third floor where he was preparing the device.

As it happened, Mr Diefenbaker, Leader of Her Majesty's Loyal
Opposition, was present in the House. There was a loud "whomp."
A number of members ran out of the Chamber. The Press Gallery
emptied. Sensing the tense atmosphere, unaware of its cause, and
evidently thinking it due to a backbench interruption, the Right
Honourable turned and demanded of his seatmate, "What did he
say, Mike? What did he say?" The *Hansard* reporter, using his own
good judgment and sense of the occasion, chose not to transcribe
the aside. The reader of *Hansard* will find the incident dealt with in
an editor's note as follows:

(*At this point a loud explosion was heard in the chamber.*)

Charles L. Empringham

A note in Chartier's handwriting was later found in one of his pockets. What he had planned to say included the following:

> Mr Speaker, Gentlemen, I might as well give you a blast to wake you up...The only bills you pass are the ones that line your pockets, while the rest of the country has to eat spaghetti and meat balls.

This, of course, was not the only throwing incident in the Commons. A few years earlier a visitor heaved a carton containing a pint or two of animal's blood into the Chamber. It sailed over the government benches, splattered the suit of at least one member, the Hon. Paul Hellyer, narrowly missed hitting a *Hansard* reporter's shoulder, and splashed all over the green carpeted floor. It was, to quote the late W. C. Fields, "the spreadin'est stuff I ever saw!"

The Great Fire of 1916

NUMEROUS accounts have been given of the great fire of 1916 which destroyed the original Parliament Buildings, except the Library, on the night of 3 February. In normal circumstances, abnormal interruptions of proceedings in the House of Commons are treated in *Hansard* with the briefest of explanatory notes, seldom over a line and a half in length. On this occasion, however, eighteen whole lines are devoted to the event.

Fisheries was the subject under debate. A Mr Loggie was pressing for better transportation facilities (this was before the advent of "reefer" or refrigeration cars). Referring to St John harbour salmon, he said:

> By the time the salmon arrive at Montreal the oil has gone out of the fish, and you see a white scum on the skin. That fish must be consumed almost immediately, as in that condition it is not up to the standard. Now if that difficulty could be got over, if the minister would be willing to take up the matter with the Railway Department, and insist that the fish be put in a car with a partition so that one end could be kept cool while the express man could have his quarters in the other compartment, the fish would arrive in Montreal in perfect condition.*

A few seconds later what arrived in the House of Commons was something much different and far more unexpected.

> At this time Mr C. R. Stewart, Chief Doorkeeper of the House of Commons, came hurriedly into the Chamber and called out: "There is a big fire in the reading room; everybody get out

Debates, 3 February 1916, p. 577.

quickly." The sitting was immediately suspended without formality, and members, officials, and visitors in the galleries, fled from the Chamber. Some of them were almost overcome by the rapidly-advancing smoke and flames before reaching a place of safety. The fire, which had originated in the reading room, gained momentum with extreme rapidity and was soon beyond control. It continued till the following day, resulting in the almost total destruction of the Parliament buildings, together with the loss of several lives.

Among those who lost their lives were two guests of the Speaker, the Hon. Albert Sévigny, who lived in an apartment in the Centre Block. A graphic account by one of the Speaker's daughters appeared in the Montreal *Gazette* as recently as 17 June 1978.* One Member of Parliament, Bowman B. Law (Yarmouth) also perished, as did Jean Baptiste Laplante, Clerk Assistant; Alphonse Desjardins and A. Desjardins, House employees; and Robert Fanning, a policeman.

It was wartime, and arson was suspected. A Royal Commission of Inquiry was immediately appointed to investigate, but its results were inconclusive. However, this was one occasion when a *Hansard* man was able to speak publicly and give his version of events. It was George Simpson, the same reporter who had set down Mr Loggie's last words and Mr Stewart's cry of "Fire." His evidence is reproduced in toto. It tells something of the man, and of the spirit of *Hansard*.

GEORGE SIMPSON, sworn:

> *By Mr White, K.C.:*
> Q. You are a Hansard reporter?—A. Yes.
> Q. And you were present in the vicinity of the reading-room the night the fire occurred?—A. Not in the vicinity of the reading-room—I was in our office just at the back of the main entrance.
> Q. Your office is separated from the main entrance by that glass partition?—A. Yes.
> Q. You were in the office?—A. If I might just tell what happened

*In the Saturday column "Of Many Things" by Edgar Andrew Collard, distinguished editor emeritus.

George Simpson

as I saw it—we have an electrical clock in our office, which marks off the ten-minute periods for each member of the Staff—that is, it marks the time each member goes on the floor—my time was 8.55; my bell rang automatically at 8.55 and at that moment I started into the Chamber, going through the door just on the east side of the east lobby—I walked through that to the door of the Chamber where the Sergeant-at-Arms sits. At that time there was no sign of any fire or smell of smoke in that corridor. I had been on the floor of the House taking notes of the member who was speaking, for approximately three or three and a half minutes, when Mr Stewart burst open the door and shouted that there was a fire in the reading-room. Just at his left was some other gentleman whom I cannot identify—there was somebody at his heels almost—they almost came in together.

Q. Then did you go out of the entrance of the Sergeant-at-Arms?—A. No, sir—when the alarm was given I waited to see what the Speaker would do, and when I saw him and the others moving, I got up and there was a general movement towards the door of the Speaker's entrance. I walked forward along as everybody did—there was no disorder, although everybody moved quickly, and I went out of the corridor opposite Room 16 to the post-office lobby, and from there I went quickly to the Senate entrance of our room to give the alarm to my confrères in the office.

Q. When you passed that eastern corridor, did you see the flame or smoke?—A. There was just this, when I heard the alarm given I turned suddenly and I saw smoke, and either flame or the reflection of flame at the northeast corner of the Commons Chamber, at the door, and I saw as the door was opened at the Sergeant-at-Arms seat, at that centre door—I saw smoke and either flame or the reflection of flame.

Q. But when you went from the post office lobby to the Senate to warn your confrères, did you see flame and smoke in the eastern corridor?—A. Yes, sir, there was a flame coming rapidly forward in the easterly corridor.

Q. Coming along these lockers?—A. Well, I did not take time to notice the details—I saw flames and smoke in there.

Q. Then you fix the alarm of fire, as nearly as possible, at 8.58?—A. Approximately that.

Q. Is there anything else you can tell us?—A. There is just one point: I saw a statement attributed to some one that the firemen did not get there for half an hour after the fire started—well, I went into our room and stayed around there for five minutes, about the entrance, while the policemen were starting the hose there. Then I was down in the vestibule and in two or three minutes some Dominion policemen got active in excluding the crowd—I went out then and remained for a couple of minutes and started down to the front gate and as I walked down I saw the firemen coming in the eastern entrance.

Q. That would be a matter of a few minutes after seeing the fire?—A. A matter of eight or nine minutes possibly.

What Simpson did not add was that with him as he walked down to the front gate was his shorthand notebook. He still had the end of Mr Loggie's speech to dictate, check, and send to the King's Printer. This he did from an hotel room nearby. So, for the guidance of future *Hansard* reporters in future parliamentary fires, George Simpson has set the precedent on behaviour: remain at your desk until the Speaker leaves the Chamber, warn your colleagues, and then get out. Above all, retain your notebook. Your work isn't finished until you have dictated the last words of the last speaking member.*

George Simpson joined the *Hansard* staff in 1899. He became Editor of Debates in 1926, ten years after the Great Fire of 1916, and relinquished the post to Earl Young in 1932. A. C. Campbell paid the following tribute to him:

It was in contemplation of one of the Simpson achievements that Hon. Mr Burrell wrote in his essay: "Hansard is better indexed than any other author that ever walked the earth."

The name Burrell has been mentioned previously. He too had a terrifying experience in the 1916 fire:

Hon. Martin Burrell, Minister of Agriculture, had a narrow escape from death. He was working with his secretary in his office off the Reading Room. When the alarm reached him he opened the door

---

*In 1979 it was discovered that an original copy of the report of the *Royal Commission re Parliament Buildings Fire*, filed with the Parliamentary Library, was missing. If anyone happens to have an original copy, perhaps donating it to the Library would commend itself to that reader.

and was met by a wall of flame. Dashing through it he fortunately made the Commons lobby, but was badly burned and it was months before he recovered from the shock. . . .

The writer of the above words was Arthur Beauchesne, who at the time of the fire was a legal officer in the Department of Justice and who, thirteen days later, was appointed Clerk Assistant of the House of Commons to succeed the unfortunate Jean Baptiste Laplante. He has since become known to generations of Canadian parliamentarians as author of *Beauchesne's Parliamentary Rules and Forms*, the standard authority, along with Bourinot, on procedure and precedent in Canadian parliamentary practice.

The Parliamentary Library survived the 1916 fire intact, thanks to the quick action of M. C. MacCormac, the librarian on duty, who, with the help of an unnamed messenger, closed the iron doors which led directly from the reading-room to the Library "before even a spark could enter."

As a matter of historical curiosity, February has been a bad month for parliamentary fires.

At about 5.30 p.m. on the 27th of February, 1792, while the Commons was sitting in Committee respecting regulations for encouraging brewing and preventing the excessive use of spirituous liquors, a report was brought in that the roof was on fire, and the House was consequently at once adjourned by the Speaker. The whole of the western part of the roof was in flames, and fell before 7 o'clock; every possible assistance was afforded by the populace; all the engines of the city attended, and an infantry regiment, with a detachment of cavalry, was despatched from the barracks to College Green. At about one o'clock in the morning the fire was got under [control] so far as to remove apprehensions of its communicating with other parts of the building. The apartment known as the House of Commons was, however, totally consumed, and in it was burned James Barry's painting of the baptism of the King of Cashel.*

---

*John T. Gilbert, *An Account of the Parliament House, Dublin, with Notices of Parliaments Held There, 1661-1800*, published in 1896. The loss of James Barry's painting was paralleled in the 1916 conflagration when the original "Fathers of Confederation" painting by Robert Harris was burned.

Workmen rebuilding the Peace Tower, 4 July 1921.

The cause of the fire in Dublin's Parliament was attributed to the actions of "a man of the name of Nesbit, a smoke-doctor," who cut holes in the walls to carry copper piping to heat the Commons. The operation was successful, but the building perished.

By an even more remarkable coincidence, on the same date, 27 February, but in the year 1933, the Reichstag was set afire in Berlin, for which Marinus van de Lubbe was convicted and beheaded.

Alphonse Desjardins

PRIME Minister Sir John S. Thompson gave Canada its annual Labour Day statutory holiday; Clerk of the House of Commons, Sir John George Bourinot, gave Canada his *Parliamentary Procedure and Practice*, an authoritative manual on parliamentary procedure; but the *Hansard* figure who had the most lasting impact on his province, his country, and on other countries too, was Alphonse Desjardins, "the founder of the credit union movement in North America."

Born in Levis, Quebec, in 1845, Desjardins was the third son in a large family that knew poverty, how to cope with it, and eventually how to escape it. For a time after an accident that injured his father and prevented him from working, Desjardins's mother became the sole household support. Toiling for others, she grew determined that her children would receive the best education her scanty means could afford. Education was to be the avenue of release, and to that end she saw to it that Alphonse spent at least one year in the College of Levis.

Like Cobbett before him, Desjardins enlisted in the army, and served in Manitoba during the Riel uprising. Afterwards he became a newspaperman in Quebec and, naturally, learned shorthand. In 1879, he secured the contract for reporting the debates in the Quebec legislature, a task he carried on for the next eleven years.

The true measure of the man's parliamentary reporting career came in 1890 when he refused to bow to ministerial pressure and expunge an embarrassing statement from the provincial *Hansard*. "I am not here to change what a member has said on the floor," was his answer. "Others heard it. If it does not come out now, what faith can there be in public documents?" Desjardins printed the statement, and was promptly damned. His reporting contract came to an end at the close of the session, and was not renewed.

Desjardins returned briefly to the newspaper profession and, eventually, in 1892, was offered, and accepted, a position as French reporter in the national Parliament at Ottawa.

In 1900 Desjardins, then in his forty-sixth year, a *Hansard* reporter on the floor of the House of Commons earning $2,000 a year, sponsored the first *caisse populaire* in the province of Quebec, in his hometown of Levis. The first deposit was the munificent sum of ten cents. Under the then provincial laws, Desjardins, as the organizer and guiding spirit, had to assume sole responsibility for any loss or defalcation. In all, about eighty venturesome souls became members, but, in five years' time, their numbers had grown greatly and the institution boasted of holding $40,000 in shares and deposits. Eighty years later, there are roughly 1,600 *caisses populaires* throughout the province of Quebec, with assets in excess of $10 billion, and across the world literally thousands of co-operatives, credit unions, societies and branches modelled on the principles laid down by Alphonse Desjardins.

Desjardins had a social conscience. He was an enemy of usury, who placed his natural talents at the service of his fellow men. During parliamentary recesses, he educated others in the efficacy of self-help. He was a contemporary of Luzatti and Griffith. In 1975 Canada honoured him by issuing a commemorative postage stamp.

In 1889, summarising his first decade as publisher of the Quebec *Hansard*, Desjardins bequeathed his credo to future generations in the following words:

> The present volume completes the first period of ten years of the existence of the Debates. Ten years. It is in every way a career for our Canadian publications of a particular character such as this. Founded in 1879, with the firm determination to make their way and to live, whatever happens, with the understanding of their usefulness being admitted, the Debates have fought all obstacles with courage and perseverance.
>
> The beginnings have been stormy and full of trouble. The sympathetic encouragement of public men, of whatever political shade, as well as the help, always so generous, which my fellow

Alphonse Desjardins

members of the Press have never ceased to grant me, here is the secret of these ten years of laborious existence.

Though short be this period, much precious material, however, has been accumulated for the history of our dear province. The Debates, with their fourteen thousand pages of parliamentary speeches, are happy to say that they will supply a large share of the information to the historian who will search for the causes of the events of which we have been witness.

To all those who have been willing to help me in a venture so new, for the efforts of a single person, and so difficult to carry out successfully, to the Press, French and English, I offer my sincere feelings of gratefulness on the closing of this first period of ten years.

The rules of the strictest impartiality will continue to be scrupulously observed in the future as in the past. The Debates record what is being spoken within the legislative halls, but they have no preference for any one. This is their main merit, and for no consideration whatever would they consent to change a line of conduct which alone can assure their existence.

As *Hansard* in the Parliament of Canada approaches its centennial, it is a cause of regret that in neither the English nor French *Hansard* offices is there to be found a portrait or photograph of Alphonse Desjardins, *Hansard* reporter, and benefactor of his fellow Canadians.

Some Toilers in the Vineyard

I T would be straining credulity to the utmost to pretend that everybody connected with the reporting of the debates in Canada's Parliament over the last hundred years was, in some measure, "a music maker, a dreamer of dreams," capable of moving and shaking the world. But each, in his or her own way, rose to the top of the reporting profession. "The cream of shorthand writers" has been the common designation of *Hansard* reporters in many jurisdictions and many lands. Their numbers are few: in Canada a mere thirteen in the Commons, in New Zealand eight, in Ireland ten, in England twenty-one. To be exceptional in such a group is a distinction.

Mention has been made of Stephen Abbott, whose *The Pyramids and Israel* intrigued not a few during the late nineteen twenties. Now living in Jerusalem is another former member of the Canadian *Hansard* staff, Roger White, acknowledged by his colleagues as one of the finest shorthand writers ever to serve his country. A native of Belleville, Ontario, he gave up a promising career as a freelance journalist to join *Hansard*, where he was for many years resident interpreter (unpaid) of the more convoluted passages occasionally occurring in the turgid effusions of a former Secretary of State for External Affairs. This was followed by a stint as official reporter with the Supreme Court of British Columbia. Still later, he turned his poetic gift to the cause of the Baha'i religion, his most recent collection of poems, entitled *Another Song, Another Season*, being greeted with critics' acclaim. From his ancestral home in County Sligo to the reaches of Canada, and now Israel, his journey, happily, is far from ended.

173

On 24 February 1921, the House of Commons paid tribute to the memory of Thomas Patrick Owens, who died while serving on *Hansard*. A former parliamentary correspondent for the Montreal *Gazette*, Owens joined the staff in the 1880s. His career was sketched in thumbnail by both the Prime Minister and the Leader of the Opposition, as the following extracts from *Hansard* show:

Right Hon. ARTHUR MEIGHEN (Prime Minister): Mr Speaker, we have learned this morning the sad news of the death of a long-standing servant of this House, the Editor of Debates, Mr Thomas P. Owens. Mr Owens was first associated with the work of Parliament as Hansard reporter not less than thirty-three years ago, and on account of his very long and excellent service I think an exception might be made to refer very briefly to him now. Previously to that, indeed, he occupied a place above your Chair, Sir, as representative of a leading Canadian newspaper. He, therefore, was virtually during the whole of his life in association with the Canadian House of Commons. He was appointed associate Editor of Debates in 1913; he became Editor of Debates in 1916; and the worth, indeed, the expertness of his services, is known and admitted by all who knew anything of his work. The warmth and geniality of his Irish character are also qualities that we shall one and all miss from this time forth, and many an hon. member of this House on either side will feel the loss of a kindly and attractive friend.

Hon. W. L. MACKENZIE KING (Leader of the Opposition): Mr Speaker, it is eminently appropriate that reference should be made to the passing of one who for many years has been a highly valued and much trusted officer of the House of Commons staff. As my right hon. friend has said, Mr T. P. Owens was associated with the staff of the House of Commons for a period of something like thirty-three years, first as a journalist, later as a reporter on the Hansard staff, and for some years past as the chief of the Hansard staff and Editor of Debates. All hon. members of the House who knew him will feel at this time a deep sense of personal loss. They will miss one who at all times was the most kindly, courteous, open-hearted and affable of men. Mr Owens held a position of great trust and responsibility. He took much pride in his work, and it was recognized, I think, by all that he brought to that important position qualities of judgment, of efficiency, of industry and of impartiality, which have helped to place the Canadian Hansard in the forefront

Thomas Patrick Owens

of the records of debates of any of the Parliaments or legislative assemblies in the world. We all deeply mourn his loss.

Tributes were also paid by the Hon. T. A. Crerar (Marquette), and later by Thomas Vien (Lotbinière).

Death, however, was not to sever completely Owens's connection with *Hansard*. On 3 March 1919, a telegram was despatched by Owens to a newspaperman in Charlottetown, Prince Edward Island, containing a message of just eight words: "Can you report at once for temporary employment?"

The recipient replied by letter the same day on the stationery of the *Charlottetown Guardian*—"Covers Prince Edward Island like the Dew". A portion of his answer reads: "If I can have an assured prospect of qualifying myself for a permanent position as a reporter on your excellent staff, by any sort of apprenticeship, I am prepared to render any and every service with a right good will and to the very best of my skill and ability, sacrificing any present ease and enduring—as my family are ready to endure—any hardship for the greater opportunity." The writer was Thomas Stephen Hubbard. Nine days later he was in Ottawa and working for the Canadian Parliament at a salary slightly below that available in PEI. Two years later he became a fully fledged *Hansard* reporter. In time he was to become the Editor of Debates in the Commons, and later, two of his sons joined the Senate reporting staff, where one of them, also named Thomas Stephen Hubbard, is currently Editor of Debates. The second son, Gil, continues as a reporter on the floor of the Senate.

Thus from Owens's telegram in 1919 has come a Hubbard family service of some sixty-one years to the Parliament of Canada, a record not likely to be approached, let alone broken, in many years to come.

When the centennial of the official Senate reporting staff is celebrated in 2016, pride of place certainly will belong to the Hubbards. They are thoroughly a *Hansard* family. Indeed, Thomas Hubbard senior's reference to "an expected domestic event" in 1919 is probably the first annunciation on file in any *Hansard* office anywhere in the world, and goes to show the worth of preserving such memoranda for the sake of posterity. As Editor, Tom

belong, unlike their colleagues of the Press, to an official staff under the authority of Mr Speaker. Suppose he claimed the right to do what he liked with his own—and to demand of them regular displays of virtuosity in construing, viva voce, their own outlines? They might be tempted to stand for Parliament—and make their own speeches.

The cast in the cameo referred to were: Mr Speaker, the Hon. W. Ross Macdonald; Prime Minister, Right Hon. Louis St. Laurent; Leader of the Opposition, Hon. George Drew; *Hansard* reporter, John Robertson; with Mr Stanley Knowles, MP (Winnipeg North Centre), Mr J. G. Diefenbaker, MP (Prince Albert), and the Hon. Douglas C. Abbott (Minister of Finance) in supporting roles. The incident took place in the afternoon and evening sessions on 13 January and is reported at pages 945 and 967 of that day's *Hansard*. Mr Robertson became Editor of Debates in 1974, and was presented with the Queen's Silver Jubilee commemorative medal on his retirement in 1977.

———

From the *Times* of London to *Time* magazine is a short hop. Six years before the Robertson incident, a *Hansard* veteran with forty-seven years' service appeared in the Canadian section of *Time*. On 12 May 1947, the news magazine quoted Miss Ida Armstrong Boyce as saying, "*Hansard* has been my life... *Hansard* is a wonderful institution." It must have seemed that way to Miss Boyce, who was twenty-four when she joined the staff in 1900, and in her seventy-first year when she retired. She served a total of twelve Parliaments, from the eighth to the twentieth and, as *Time* recorded:

It was a monotonous task [taking dictation from a reporter], but Ida seldom found it dull as ministers came & went and the country fought two wars. She remembers the earthiness of onetime Agriculture Minister William Motherwell, whose language sometimes stretched the limits of parliamentary proprieties and whose favourite epithet was "heifer dust." She remembers, from the days when there was no 40-minute limit on speeches, how she recorded orations that sometimes lasted eight hours.

Miss Boyce was the daughter of John C. Boyce, assistant to the first *Hansard* Chief Reporter in 1880. Her brother, Charles Boyce, also worked on *Hansard* before joining the Journals branch of the House of Commons.

––––––––––––––––

George B. Bradley was the first *Hansard* Chief Reporter, and served from 1880 until the last year of the century. Eighty years later, on 24 April 1979, his name surfaced once more, in the pages of the Montreal *Gazette*.

Bradley had been a newspaperman before he was chosen to head that first staff. It is worth recalling that in its early years Parliament sat for just a few months each year, and that during recesses and elections Bradley and his colleagues were free to engage in other work. Being an expert shorthand reporter and experienced journalist, it was only natural that Bradley should return to his former profession during such periods, one of which was the general election of 1887.

> The newspaper reporter of Victorian days had a far harder time getting a scoop written for a deadline. Rapid communication by telephone or telegraph might not be available. He himself had to get back to his office, frequently by slow, uncertain travel, and then write out his story by longhand. As he finished each sheet it might be snatched from him to be set up in type, while he scribbled the rest. . . .
>
> Another *Gazette* reporter, George Bradley, was sent that winter [1887] to cover a big election rally at Chambly, only a few days before the polling. After the meeting, he headed for Montreal in a sleigh. The horses gave out in the drifts. Bradley took to snowshoes. He crossed the St Lawrence by Victoria Bridge.
>
> At that time the bridge was for trains only, without any walkway for foot passengers. Bradley had to take his chances that no train would come during the two-mile tramp above the river. The bridge

was then covered, like a tunnel, and pitch black. He had to grope his way along.

Bradley emerged at the Montreal end only to find drifts everywhere and no cabs to be seen. He had to snowshoe from Pointe St Charles to the *Gazette* office, then on Craig St., behind the Place d'Armes post office. But he got his story written and just in time.*

As these words are being written, three jet aircraft, hired by the three major political parties, are criss-crossing Canada, carrying media representatives covering the 1979 general election. One of the stories of the campaign is how the reporters' baggage is being tenderly and lovingly shepherded from point to point, lest a stray bag result in one discomfited journalist. George Bradley must be chuckling as he observes the spectacle, leaning against some white powdery bank, with his snowshoes strapped across his shoulders, looking down from Heaven.†

Not all the people of *Hansard* were fortunate enough to reach merited retirement years. One of the more recent casualties was Lucien R. Guertin, Editor of French Debates, who died on 3 October 1973, while still in his fifties. A man of drive and initiative, his work in helping to establish the Canadian Hansard Association is remembered by those first delegates from the various provincial legislatures across Canada who assembled in Ottawa in the summer of 1973. The hospitality of his home in Hull, Quebec, was always extended with a warm heart to all in the shorthand reporting fraternity.

Although not of the *Hansard* family, another group of people in Hull have been so long associated with the production of *Hansard* that failure to acknowledge their dedication and co-operation in ensuring a trouble-free operation would be remiss. They are the

*Edgar Andrew Collard, "Newspaper Scoops", in *The Gazette*, 24 April 1979.

†The 1887 election took place in mid-winter. As this book is going to press, Canada is experiencing another winter election, the first since Bradley's time.

men and women of the Government Printing Bureau, upon whose labours members and the general public rely for the prompt publication and delivery of the daily issue when Parliament is in session. Surprisingly, in all the many works, articles and manuscripts dealing with Canada's *Hansard* over the past hundred years, there has been little, indeed hardly any, reference made to those who print it and who, over the years, have displayed an abiding commitment to making the record as error free as possible. The following incident is not an uncommon example of that commitment.

It is 3.15 in the morning. A working *Hansard* editor has just reached his home in Nepean after a drive of almost an hour through snowdrifts along the Ottawa River Parkway, normally a fifteen-minute run. There is no sound outside or inside the sleeping household. Then the telephone rings. It is the Printing Bureau. They have spotted an error, a wrong name, an incorrect designation. Mr X has been shown as replying on behalf of a minister, sometime during the day's sitting from 2 p.m. until 10.30 p.m. But Mr X was replaced by Mr Y as parliamentary secretary ten days ago. "We think it's a mistake. Can you check it out?"

Gaston Lapointe, Robert Tessier, and Bob Martin have been on the job once more, and to them and their confrères in the Printing Bureau, *Hansard* and the Parliament of Canada are indebted. Ed Phillips, one of the few remaining "hot metal" veterans of another era, successfully coping with computerized word-processing and all that it entails, also deserves our thanks.

Earl Courtney Young was born in Charlottetown, Prince Edward Island, in 1890. His father was a schoolteacher. After leaving Prince of Wales College, he became a reporter on the *Charlottetown Guardian*, as always covering PEI "like the dew," and taught himself shorthand, a rather remarkable accomplishment in itself. In later years he was "clocked at 263 words a minute in short spurts," an essential requirement for a competent *Hansard* reporter sans tape, mechanical recording and playback apparatus. Shorthand was his entry, first to court reporting and later to the

Earl Courtney Young

post of official reporter for the PEI legislature. In 1912 he was one of three successful candidates in the first civil service competition held to fill positions on *Hansard* in the Canadian Parliament.

A year later, in 1913, came an event of some moment in Canadian parliamentary history. For two weeks, from each Monday to the following Saturday, the House sat in continuous session; this was the notorious "naval debate filibuster." The First World War was approaching. The Prime Minister, Sir Robert Borden, proposed that Canada contribute $35 million, a large amount in those days, to the purchase of ships by the British navy. The Liberal opposition opposed Borden's bill, launched an all-out filibuster, more reminiscent of American Senate practice than the Canadian tradition and, at the end of two weeks, succeeded in having the measure beaten down. Also beaten down physically were certain members of the House and its staff, including *Hansard* reporters. At the time there were eight of them and one editor, Albert Horton. Two of the reporters were French shorthand writers, J. O. Marceau and Alphonse Desjardins. Of the other five, Young was the youngest.

The mechanics chosen by the *Hansard* staff to cope with the filibuster seem simple in retrospect. The older members reported the proceedings during the day, and the younger men took over in the evening and during the night. It was a tremendous undertaking, and took its toll in ill health. Within a few years none of the original staff remained on strength. The closest parallel in modern times came in the early 1960s when five reporters carried out the daily reporting of the Debates for one full session.

Earl Young also experienced the Great Fire of 1916. He was one of those in the *Hansard* office who were warned by George Simpson to get out. Young did not get out of *Hansard* until 1952, after a service of forty years. He was a noted golfer and skier, and had been a member of the Chartered Shorthand Reporters Association of Ontario, the Editors and Public Relations Group of the Professional Institute of the Civil Service, and the Canadian Institute of International Affairs.

Young was not the only *Hansard* man to serve and support the Professional Institute of the Public Service of Canada (PIPS). In 1922 Albert Horton, then of the Senate Debates staff, became the first chairman of the editors' group, and in 1923 A. C. Campbell of the Commons Debates staff was chosen as editor of the Institute's *Bulletin*. It was as the result of the work of the editors' group that a style book was drawn up to provide uniformity of treatment for all government publications. In his *The Story of the Professional Institute 1920-1945*, J. Stuart McGiffin paid fulsome tribute to Campbell on the latter's death in November 1943.

———

There are many other people associated with *Hansard* over the past one hundred years who are deserving of recognition in this chronicle. Within the constraints applicable to a quondam serving officer of the House, however, not to mention a pressing publication deadline, much has had perforce to be filed away for future endeavour. A bicentennial chronicler may then do justice to those overlooked here, and the names of Percy Shelton, Bill Clinton, Hughie Huggins, Don Butt, Don Coghill, Kirk Crockett, and a host of others will find their respective and respected places.

At the end of this book is appended a *Hansard* Roll of Honour, listing the names of all those House of Commons reporters who have written shorthand "in the cause of their country" over the last century. It was prepared by Mrs Betty Mae Stacey and Miss Sally Jarbeau, *Hansard* amanuenses, to whom acknowledgment is gratefully made. Regrettably, there is no complete record of all the women who served as amanuenses, and as indexing and revising clerks, during those hundred years. Although inadequate, the list which follows at least gives the names of presently serving personnel to whom must go much of the credit for *Hansard*'s reputation as a reputable and reliable parliamentary history: Betty Anderson, Lucy Frost, Evelyn Conley, Pat Logan, Irene Bennett, Hazel Robinson, Chrystine Carroll, Teresa Fuller, Grace Soublière, Kathleen Snow, Joan Kuffner, Joyce Sellars, Peggy Gillespie, Anita St Amour and Ray Boucher. In addition, there are those who run the in-office printing unit, and the indispensable pages and messengers "of winged foot," whose frequent forays in search of MP's notes and quotations contribute to the smooth running of the operation. These include Allan O'Connor, Clifford

Parmeter, Jean-Yves Momy, James Ward, Paul Devine, André Marion, Robert Allen, Jimmy Petrow and Richard Davis.

In French Debates the unsung staff, many with long tenure, include Dominique Blais, Carmen Bourgeau, Pierette Charlebois, Huguette Côté, Yvette Dionne, Ghislaine Labelle, Donald Loiselle, Rita Lupien, Denise Séguin, Marlene Waters, Marcel Brault, Marcel Brunet, Albert Faucher, Bernard Latulippe, David Lavictoire and Maurice Poirier.

Should there by any omission, or inclusions not desired, in any of the foregoing pages, this chronicler asks forgiveness. His alone has been the responsibility.

A Brief History of Shorthand

I T is a far cry from the city of Ottawa in 1980 to the ancient city of Caesarea in Palestine in 260 A.D., but in Caesarea over seventeen hundred years ago was born Eusebius Pamphili, "the father of ecclesiastical history—the first, the only historian of the Church bordering on primitive times." Eusebius published in 312 A.D. the first chapters of his *The History of the Church from Christ to Constantine*, described by one authority as "the only work of its kind, possessing a value to subsequent ages which belongs to no other uninspired work."

His relevance to this book, however, grows from his authoritative reference in Book VI, Chapter XXIII, to the use of shorthand in the second and third centuries of the Christian era:

> Starting from that time also Origen's commentaries on the divine Scriptures had their beginning, at the instigation of Ambrose, who not only plied him with innumerable verbal exhortations and encouragements, but also provided him unstintingly with what was necessary. For as he dictated there were ready at hand more than seven shorthand-writers, who relieved each other at fixed times, and as many copyists, as well as girls skilled in penmanship; for all of whom Ambrose supplied without stint the necessary means. Nay further, he contributed to Origen* a vast amount of zeal in the earnest study of the divine oracles, a zeal which more than anything else acted as an incentive to him to compose his commentaries.

For eighty years, from 1880 until 1964, "seven shorthand-writers," relieving "each other at fixed times," reported the

---

*Origen was an early Christian martyr. "A Greek, educated in Greek learning," he was born c. 186 A.D. and died in 254 A.D. as a result of torture received during persecution.

Debates in the Canadian House of Commons. In the latter year their number was increased by two. The names of the first seven so engaged are herewith given: George B. Bradley, Stephen A. Abbott, E. Joseph Duggan, George Eyvel, Albert Horton, F.R. Marceau, and Thos. Jno. Richardson.

The written history of shorthand extends over two thousand years. There have been a number of excellent works that trace its development, but two authorities spring readily to mind, E. H. Butler and Alexander Tremaine Wright. Unfortunately, their books are long out of print, and rare copies can be found only with difficulty.

Many attempts have been made to pinpoint the earliest known references to "the winged art," and the surmising imperative has been used by some hardy souls to give it biblical connotation. Yet, those who seek to interpret scriptural writings in this way do a disservice, although no doubt they are motivated by the most sincere intentions. There is no such need, given the vast quantity of other source material.

In sum, shorthand is compressed writing. Its development almost paralleled that of the alphabet itself. There have been many alphabets devised for many tongues, and for every one, an hundred and more shorthand systems. The International Shorthand Congress held in London in 1887 took note—no pun intended—of no fewer than 482 systems. Since then, in English alone, well over another hundred systems have been introduced.

There is no mystery about shorthand. Anybody can write it, can invent a shorthand system, and can adapt or improve an existing system to meet special circumstances. Before the advent of typewriters, every newspaperman had to "longhand" his reports and articles, and this gave rise in itself to an almost universal "short" longhand, readily understood by reporter, sub-editor and compositor. Examples of the simpler variants included "wd" for would, "cd" for could, "shd" for should, "tt" for that, "t" for the. Simplicity was its essence, but came the day when "sub." and "comp." were completely baffled to meet "tbs" in a report dealing with matters ecclesiastic. "Pray, elucidate", or some such phrase, was their query. "Why, transubstantiation, of course," replied the scribe. It is recorded that shortly thereafter, to be exact, the following payday, he himself was "tbs-d" and later became a shoe salesman—in short, an "s-s".

Shorthand is the principal tool of the *Hansard* reporter. Today that shorthand can be written by hand, with pen and ink, or pencil, or it may be imprinted mechanically by a palantype or stenotype machine. Something to write with, and something to write on, are all that are needed by the professional shorthand writer to make a living in any part of the globe.

Rushes or reeds were the first scribes' pens. They were sliced to make a chisel-faced nib, the broad side of which was used to write thick strokes, and the other side to make thin lines. The quill pen, as advanced in its day as the fountain pen or ballpoint, was a Greek invention, circa 300 B.C. It continued in use for well over two thousand years, the quill itself eventually being fitted with a metal tip to obviate constant trimming and resharpening. Selection of the feathered quill was all-important. A reference by P. J. Dowling, in his book *The Hedge Schools of Ireland*, to one teacher's preference for "dutchified quills" in 1793 appears to indicate that the geese of Holland must have been valued as much for the quality of their feathers as for their eggs and flesh.

The quill pen was, of course, a dip pen: its user needed a bottle of ink at hand into which he would dip his pen after writing a line or two. It might seem that this constant lifting of the pen from paper to bottle, and back again, would rob the shorthand writer of speed. Surprisingly, as late as the early 1960s, one professional shorthand reporter, Barry Shields of Vancouver, was demonstrating that this was not so. While others would enter a courtroom festooned with tape recorders, microphones, a tangle of wires and assorted plugs, the most expensive ballpoint pens, and so on, the unflappable Shields would produce his little bottle of ink, his dip pen and pad, and proceed to make expert court reports, as though the technology of the twentieth century were still aeons away.

An interesting footnote on the development of the pen turned up during the collecting of material for another portion of this book. Samuel Thompson, whose story is briefly given elsewhere, devoted a chapter of his book, *Reminiscences of a Canadian Pioneer*, to his maternal uncle John Isaac Hawkins "descended from Sir John Hawkins, the world-renowned buccaneer, admiral, and founder of the English Royal Navy." Dr Hawkins—civil engineer, inventor, poet, preacher, phrenologist, preserver in spirits of the heart and windpipe of his naturally deceased, unnaturally adopted, son—had invented the "ever-pointed pencil," and the "iridium-pointed gold pen."

Many of the present generation of *Hansard* reporters began their working careers using a fountain pen, and several still prefer it. However, it has been largely supplanted by the ballpoint pen, an invention that swept the world shortly after the Second World War. Its introduction was a cause of wonderment wherever it appeared. Initially it was a most expensive pen, affordable only to the wealthy. Of course, the first ballpoints were produced before the era of planned obsolescence, and were guaranteed to give years of service.

Having dwelt overly on pens, the other necessity of the scribe, "something to write on," can be dealt with briefly. Egyptian papyrus was the first material to gain wide acceptance. Made from reeds, it was the forerunner of today's paper. Clay tablets were used in earlier times, and reusable wax tablets were much in vogue in the early Roman empire. Museums and archives the world over contain many samples of these materials. The little-known National Postal Museum in Ottawa is worth a visit solely for the purpose of seeing its exhibit of letters written in clay, sealed in baked clay envelopes, and safely carried by mailmen over prodigious distances in Persia 3,000 years ago.

As has been said, shorthand itself came into being almost contemporaneously with longhand. The reason is not far to seek. It takes but little imagination to conjure up an irate ruler, or teacher, dictating to a scribe, hampered by an unwieldy, cumbersome alphabet: "Dammit, man! Can't you go faster?" And the scribe would have been well advised to try. Thus came the dropping of certain superfluous or repetitive symbols, and, of necessity, the birth of shorthand.

The dropping of unnecessary symbols continues to this very day. The *Hansard* reporter who hears the phrase "in my constituency" time without number, soon learns or devises a more abbreviated shorthand symbol than is normal, even in the high-speed systems used by parliamentary reporters. If you, dear reader, have pen and paper, try this experiment. Make a small circle—O. Now put a dot in it—⊙. Do it ten times, each time faster than the preceding one— ⊙ ⊙ ⊙ ⊙ ⊙ ⊙ ⊙ ⊙ ⊙ ⊙. Now, as your write it, say "in my constituency," "in my constituency," "in my constituency." There is no way you can say "in my constituency" as fast as you write "⊙" Welcome to the shorthand club.

And what system of shorthand is this? "Well, you see, the circle is the boundary of the constituency, and the dot is the little man standing inside it!" The writer is forever indebted to the late Peggy Fitzgerald, official reporter, Dáil Eireann, for this shortcut that has stood him in good stead this past quarter century. It is the Fitzgerald over-drive technique.

Early Systems of Shorthand

T HERE is sound reason for ascribing the invention of shorthand to the Greeks, and for its adoption professionally to the
Egyptians, followed by the Romans. Tiro, a slave in Rome, and
Cicero's amanuensis, is generally credited with the development of
the Tironian notae, of which more than four thousand symbols
were in use before the birth of Christ. Many were arbitrary in
nature, akin to our old friend, "in my constituency," while others
had a definite syllabic basis, capable of adaptation to new words
and phrases.

It is recorded that Tiro, or to give him his full name, Marcus
Tullius Tiro, was made a freeman as a reward for his work. Over
the succeeding twenty centuries his work made shorthand slaves of
hundreds of thousands of freeborn men and women as they strove
to master its complexities and to become proficient writers and
reporters.

Some of the most noted early practitioners of shorthand writing
included Cicero, Julius Caesar and Augustus. Bishops of the
Church were quick to recognize its worth. By the second century,
shorthand schools were not uncommon. One papyrus record
contains details of a contract to teach shorthand in Egypt in 155
A.D.

John Robert Gregg, born in Rockcorry, County Monaghan, in
1867, inventor of the shorthand system that bears his name, has
given us the following story which illustrates the progress of
shorthand in Rome in the second century A.D.:

Marcus Aurelius Clemens Prudentius, the most famous of the
Roman Christian poets in the third century, expressed regret at the
unhappy fate of the shorthand-writer reporting a trial in court. The

centurion Metellus, having been converted to Christianity, refused to perform some of his duties as a Roman soldier; he was what we should now term a "conscientious objector." Metellus asked a fellow Christian who was a shorthand-writer, to report the trial of his case. When the judge decided the case against Metellus and condemned him to death, the shorthand-writer flung his tablets at the head of the judge. His subsequent fate is told in the laconic statement, "By order of the judge, he was torn to pieces."

Indeed, shorthand reporting was among the most hazardous of professions in Rome. Severus, who was Emperor from 193 to 211 A.D., went so far as to command that any shorthand-writer reporting a court case and making a mistake, "should have the tendons of his right hand severed, and . . . be banished [from] the Empire for life."

With Rome's decline, the use of shorthand grew less and less. The arbitrary Tironian notes had grown to almost 15,000 by the sixth century, an almost impossible number to memorize. But elsewhere, in other tongues and in later centuries, people still persisted in speed writing, experimenting, modelling, adapting:

The earliest English alphabet of a stenographic nature was invented by a monk, John of Tilbury, who wrote an epistle on the notarial art, addressed to King Henry II, about 1180. Each letter consisted of a vertical line, with a short horizontal stroke placed around in various positions, and from this he obtained eighteen characters, some of which look very much like a child's crude drawings of railway signals. John of Tilbury also used a dot in several positions around the vertical stroke to represent the *amo, amas, amat, amamus, amatis* and *amant* of the Latin grammar, while the vertical stroke with a semicircle attached gave him *amabam* and *amabamus*. This portion of his scheme has a resemblance to four other works published centuries afterwards, including Dr Timothe Bright's shorthand and George Dalgarno's *Universal Language*, which is often quoted as an early attempt to provide a universal sign language on the lines of Esperanto and Occidental.*

*E.H. Butler, *The Story of British Shorthand* (London: Sir Isaac Pitman & Sons Ltd., 1951), p. 5.

The mention of Esperanto is fortuitous but of some relevance to this chronicle. L. L. Zamenhof was the originator of Esperanto, the one common denominator linguistic shorthand to succeed in the twentieth century, spoken in almost every country in the world, a language which knows neither race nor nation, universal and world-binding in concept and usage. Its effectiveness is beyond question. People of twelve nationalities meeting together, speak with one tongue, understood by all. Esperanto, like shorthand, is a man-made thing, a communication device based on scientific principles. As such, it exercises a magnetic quality for the shorthand purist, and a prime example of the latter is Lorcan O hUiginn, former *Hansard* reporter in the Senate of Canada, past president of the Esperanto Association of Canada, adapter of Pitman shorthand to the Irish language, and currently in the process of collecting materials for a Universal Stenographic Museum with branches in Ottawa and Dublin.

Mention has already been made of father and son shorthand teams, and standing high on the list is that of the O hUiginn family. Even before his tenth birthday, the son had already absorbed the first principles of Pitman from his father, Bernard, who ran the Emerald Standard Shorthand School in Dublin. The son became an official reporter of debates in Dáil Eireann, meantime acquiring the start of a life-long interest in Esperanto. The combination of the two skills, one written, one spoken, made him a world traveller, instantly at home in any corner of the globe.

According to *Haydn's Dictionary of Dates*, Dr Timothe Bright published the first English work on shorthand in 1588. Entitled *Characterie, or the Arte of Shorte, Swifte and Secrete Writing*, it enjoyed wide vogue. Among his pupils were Sir Robert Cecil, and a Miss Jane Seager, described by Butler as "the first known lady shorthand-writer," at least in England. A sample of her work, executed in 1589, is preserved in the British Museum. As will be mentioned later, samples of a Nova Scotian lady's shorthand, written in 1867, three hundred years later, are to be found in the Public Archives of Canada.

The Art of Stenographie, published in 1602 by the Rev. John Willis, is generally regarded as the forerunner of modern shorthand systems. His syllabic abbreviations made commonsense, and the principles he enunciated were followed by several shorthand innovators and inventors in succeeding years. Some thirty years later a certain Theophilus Metcalfe produced a system called "Radio-stenography, Short Writing." The title alone places it in the category of the curious.

In 1742 John Byrom, a Mancunian, secured passage of an Act of Parliament granting him the right to teach his own system of shorthand, and in 1750 Thomas Gurney's *Brachygraphy*, was published, thus launching a famous shorthand reporting firm that is still active over two hundred years later. The novelist, Charles Dickens, was employed on a part-time basis by the Gurney establishment to assist in reporting debates at Westminster. At the time he was only eighteen years old, and used the experience to some advantage later.*

A comparison of Gurney's parliamentary committee reporting with present-day committee reporting in the Canadian House of Commons is of great interest. The following is taken from W. J. Carlton's *Charles Dickens, Shorthand Writer*, wherein he details that in 1824 the establishment of William Brodie Gurney consisted of "four constant clerks."

> In 1833, giving evidence before a Select Committee on House of Commons Offices and Fees, he [Gurney] stated that, in addition to his two sons and an assistant, he employed other shorthand writers, not in his own office, when the number of committees was such as to require it, "having sometimes to provide for twelve Committees of the House on the same day." It is possible that Dickens may occasionally have reported one of these committees.

Nelson R. Butcher of Toronto assisted in supplying extra reporting assistance to the Ottawa committee's branch for many

---

*The opening chapter of *The Pickwick Papers* satirises parliamentary manners. Sir Andrew Agnew's bill to outlaw all recreation for "the lower classes" on Sundays, supported by Dr Blomfield, the Bishop of London, gave rise to the creation of the hypocritical Stiggins, precursor of Uriah Heep. Fitzkin and Slumkey, "slinging violent political abuse," were also based on Dickens's observations of parliament and politics. See Edgar Johnson, *Charles Dickens: His Tragedy and Triumph* (Harmondsworth: Penguin Books, 1979), p. 110.

years, as did another veteran Canadian reporter, Frank Nethercut, in the days before the introduction of tape recording. The savings to the Canadian taxpayer were huge.

Before leaving Gurney, it is also worth noting that the shorthand reporter remained at his post throughout the duration of a meeting. At half-hourly intervals he received a fresh notebook from a messenger, who returned to the office with the previous half hour's shorthand, which was then read and dictated to two longhand transcribers by a clerk skilled in reading the reporter's shorthand. Some stenotype court and conference reporters adopt the same procedure even today.

The Flight of the Eagle Quill

THE nineteenth century was the golden era of shorthand invention. "A Pen Plucked from an Eagle's Wing," one of the systems published in the seventeenth century by William Mason, was in keeping with the synonym for shorthand, "the winged art," and now the "Eagle Quill" was to take flight, from country to country, continent to continent.

Between 1800 and 1900 well over two-hundred and fifty books dealing with various shorthand systems are catalogued. One wonders about the fate of the following random selection: *A New System* by Samuel Richardson (1800); *Stenographia (Welsh)* by Robert Everett (1816); *Manual of Shorthand* by J. Kelly (1820); *Parliamentary System of Shorthand Simplified* by Thomas Parker (1833); *Concise and Practical System of Stenography* by George B. Bradley (1843); *Three Systems of Shorthand* by John Price (1855); *Shorthand Swift as Speech* by John Thompson (1863); *Shorthand in a Day* by William Passmore (1870); *Phonetics of the Gaelic Language, with a System of Phonography* by Malcolm MacFarlane (1889), and *Swiftograph* by Frederick Fant Abbott (1893). Alas for Frederick Fant Abbott and the others, three titans emerged whose worth has proved enduring.

Pitman, Duployé, and Gregg gave the world modern shorthand. Since their day the only invention of note has been the introduction of machine shorthand, the credit for which is given by Haydn to an Italian, Signor A. Michela, and which was successfully adopted by the Italian Senate for the reporting of its debates. Signor Michela placed his invention, described as "like a harmonium with a keyboard," on display at the Turin Exhibition of 1884.

There were two Pitman brothers involved in shorthand, Isaac and Benn. The former is the better known. Born in 1813, he lived for eighty-five years, and was knighted by Victoria in 1894, three years before his death. An apprentice in a cloth factory at age thirteen, he studied shorthand in the little spare time he had after a twelve-hour working day. After six years in the factory, he broke away to become trained as a teacher, taught shorthand, wrote a textbook on the subject, had his manuscript rejected for publication, and was advised to devise a new system of his own.

At this stage there is a story within a story to be told. The shorthand which Isaac Pitman had learned, and which he taught, was an adaptation of an earlier system invented by Samuel Taylor (1749-1811). Taylor was a most unusual man. He was said to have had an abrasive personality, and did not suffer fools gladly, as the following quotation illustrates:

> Since the first introduction of the art of short-hand writing into this country, it has undergone many alterations, and of late years has been wonderfully tossed about. Those who have had the handling (or *improving*, as they say) of it, have known little or nothing of the matter, and consequently have rendered their *improvements* more complex than the originals which they pretend to have improved.*

Isaac Pitman's rejected manuscript was itself a treatise on Taylor's shorthand, and from the foregoing we know what Taylor himself would have thought of Pitman's efforts. In fact, when later he had devised his own system, Pitman was condemned by many Taylor writers for plagiarism.

In 1786 Taylor published his *Universal System of Stenography*, or to give its full title, *An Essay Intended to Establish a Standard for an Universal System of Stenography*.

It is to Taylor that we are indebted for one of the earliest examples of shorthand used in reporting parliamentary debates. One of the plates illustrating his book contains "some proceedings in the first session of the Fourth Parliament of Ireland, as taken down in short-hand in the House of Commons, on Wednesday October 29th, 1783, by the Author of this Work."

Isaac Pitman's next venture into print was in 1837, with the

---

*Samuel Taylor, *An Essay Intended to Establish a Standard for an Universal System of Stenography or Short Hand Writing* (London: J. Bell, 1786), p. 8.

publication of *Stenographic Sound-Hand*, and for the next fifty-seven years he spent himself promoting, handling and improving the system to which he gave his name. Indeed, forgetting Taylor's dictum, he continued his "improving," to such an extent that many writers refused to accept any later versions than his tenth edition, including his brother Benn, who popularised the system in the United States during the latter half of the nineteenth century.

In 1879 Pitman shorthand was adapted to Japanese, and was used for reporting debates in the Diet, the Japanese Parliament.

In 1913 one Pitman devotee was to write:

A moment's reflection will show that Isaac Pitman's achievement is unique, and that its success has been phenomenal. The majority of the systems of English shorthand have passed into oblivion, or are practised only by a few, while the method of writing for which the world is indebted to his genius has come into universal use. In the United Kingdom, except in the most thinly populated parts, it is everywhere taught; it is practised in Africa, wherever the English language has penetrated; in India votaries of the art are found from Colombo to the Himalayas; in Australia Phonography has been taught and practised as long as in the old country. Across the Atlantic we find the method held in high esteem both in Canada and in the United States, and universally employed; in South America it is in general use in Spanish adaptations. What is said of the British Empire may be said of Pitman's Phonography—the sun never sets upon it.*

In 1980 the sun still does not set upon the use of Pitman shorthand. Peter Pitman, great grandson of Sir Isaac, wrote in December 1979:

. . . we have recently been training several groups of parliamentary reporters for the new Parliaments in Nigeria. With the end of military rule it has been necessary to provide quite a large number of reporters and we have been fortunate in having the assistance of the Hansard staff in London in training them.†

*Alfred Baker, *The Life of Sir Isaac Pitman*, centenary edition (London: Sir Isaac Pitman & Sons Ltd., 1913), p. 331.

†In a letter to the author, 13 December 1979.

To give honour where honour is due, Taylor's shorthand had been adapted to a number of languages many years earlier, one incident recorded by the historian Alexander Tremaine Wright being given as follows:

> At the outset of its French career, the system obtained a public advertisement of much importance then, and of some historical interest now. Paris was enduring the throes of revolution, Louis XVI in duress was yielding to the demands of the population, events were hurrying along to the massacre of thousands and to the expulsion of tens of thousands of priests, when one Jean Jérôme Roussel was admitted to the bar of the Assemblée Nationale Legislative at their evening sitting on the 25th June, 1792, to present a petition with reference to—Taylor's Stenography!

From Paris during the French Revolution, to Kamloops, British Columbia, a hundred years later, may appear too great a distance to take in one stride, but shorthand is compression and, as with Taylor and Pitman, knows no national boundaries. Taylor gave France one system of shorthand; in turn France gave Canada and many other countries another system. In this case it is easier to tell the story from the Canadian end, beginning with the Rare Books section of the Public Archives of Canada. There the visitor will see displayed the fruits of one of the most venturesome and successful applications of shorthand ever attempted: a bound volume of issues of the *Kamloops Wawa.*

The foundation of the *Kamloops Wawa* can be traced back to the publication of a new system of shorthand by the Abbé Émile Duployé, Curé of Montigny-en-Arrouaise, in 1862. Adapted to English by an enterprising Chicagoan, Alfonzo Joseph Pernin, it became known as Duployan shorthand, and in 1881 a Scot, John Matthew Sloan, made another adaptation which in time became familiarly known as Sloan-Duployan.

James Constantine Pilling describes the first issue of the *Wawa* (2 May 1891) as follows:

> A periodical in the Chinook Jargon, stenographic characters, intended as a weekly, but issued in its early stages at irregular intervals, at Kamloops, British Columbia, under the editorship of Father Le Jeune . . .

The first three numbers are in triple columns, Jargon in italics, Jargon in shorthand characters, and English in italics; the fourth number is in double columns, Jargon in shorthand and English in italics; the subsequent issues are in shorthand with headings in English.*

Fortunately Father Le Jeune left his own account of the work:

The Duployan system of stenography made its apparition in France in 1867. The originators are the Duployé brothers, two of whom are members of the clergy and two others eminent stenographers in Paris. Father Le Jeune became acquainted with the system in 1871, being then 16 years old, and learned in a few hours. Two or three days after he wrote to Mr E. Duployé and by return mail received a very encouraging letter. He found the knowledge of shorthand very profitable ever since, either for taking down notes or for correspondence. It was only in July, 1890, that the idea first came to try the shorthand as an easy phonetic writing for the Indians of British Columbia. The first trial became a success. At the end of September, 1890, a poor Indian cripple, named Charley-Alexis Mayoos, from the Lower Nicola, saw the writing for the first time, and got the intuition of the system at first sight. He set to decipher a few pages of Indian prayers in shorthand. In less than two months he learned every word of them, and he soon began to communicate his learning to his friends and relatives.

Through his endeavors some eight or ten Indians at Coldwater, Nicola, B.C., became thoroughly acquainted with the writing system before April 1st, 1891. In July, 1891, the first lessons were given to the Shushwap Indians; they lasted an hour every day for four or five days. Three or four of the best young men went on studying what they had learned, and were delighted to find themselves able to correspond in shorthand in the early fall. During the winter months they helped to propagate the system of writing among their people. In the meantime Mayoos had come to Kamloops and was pushing the work ahead among the young people there.

In December, 1891, the system was introduced to the North Thomson Indians; in January, 1892, to those at Douglas Lake; in

*J.S. Pilling, *Bibliography of the Chinookan Languages* (Washington: Smithsonian Institution, 1893), p. 45.

February at Spuzzum and North Bend; and, last of all, in March, to those at Deadman's Creek, near Sarvina. Soon after, Indian letters came from William's Lake. In May, 1892, a few lessons were given at St Mary's Mission to the Lower Fraser and seacoast Indians. Now the Indians teach each other and are very anxious to learn on all sides. The most advanced understand the value of the letters and the spelling of the words; but the greatest number begin by reading the words, then learn the syllables by comparing the words together, and at last come to the letters. They learn by analysis and much quicker than by synthesis.

In 1896, and again in 1904, Father Le Jeune* and a number of his native Canadian pupils travelled to France where, in international shorthand competitions, the latter won, on the first occasion, one gold medal, and, on the second trip, no fewer than three gold and many silver medals.

Sloan-Duployan continued to have its adherents on the other side of the Atlantic until well past the middle of the present century. A few years before his death in 1929, Sloan claimed that his was the only system then being taught in Newfoundland. Thus, from one end of Canada to the other, in the annals of shorthand it can be clearly written, "Duployé was here."

Dr John Robert Gregg was the third man of the nineteenth century to achieve world-wide recognition through the invention of a shorthand system. Gregg is a script system, unlike Pitman and Duployan which are geometric in design. There are, however, certain similarities to be noted in the careers of both Gregg and Isaac Pitman. Each originally learned an adaptation of Taylor's *Stenography*, and each was accused of basing his system on the work of others, in Gregg's case this being "Script Phonography," invented by Thomas S. Malone, a Dublin man, who befriended Gregg and helped launch his career in the shorthand world.

Gregg was an early recruit to shorthand, learning to write it when he was only ten years of age. For the next seventy years he was occupied in writing it, modifying it, and in publishing and

*Father Jean-Marie Raphael Le Jeune was born in Pleybert Christ, Finistère, France, in April 1855. He came to British Columbia as an Oblate missionary in October 1879. He died on 21 November 1930 at Westminster, B.C.

promoting his own system which first appeared in April 1888, and which at the time he called "Light-line Phonography." Five years later he emigrated to the United States where his system was registered simply as Gregg shorthand; eventually it was taught from coast to coast. He died on 24 February 1948.

It was in the United States that the most successful advance was made in the field of machine shorthand. In 1910, Ward Stone Ireland patented the Stenotype machine which has survived the test of time. Another American machine is the Stenograph.

A French woman, Mme. Palanque, was the inventor of the Palantype machine in 1939. Since then its use has spread throughout the world, its keyboard readily lending itself to the recording of many languages. The writer recalls the late Miss Beryl Chadwick of the Canadian committee staff telling of an occasion when she was required to report some Chinese and produced an accurate phonetic transcript, using the Palantype. An even earlier example of its versatility was given by a graduate of the Palantype College of London, in the late 1940s, who was able to report speeches in Irish verbatim in Dáil Eireann, although she did not know the language.

Any day that the House of Commons is sitting in Ottawa, visitors may see the Palantype being used to report the debates by one of its most professionally competent operators, Ita Straszak. As the pioneer machine shorthand *Hansard* reporter in Canada, indeed for many years the only woman on an otherwise all-male staff, she has earned an unique niche in the annals chronicling the legislative history of her adopted country.

———

Before leaving the subject of shorthand, there is one general summation to be made, partly in answer to the almost inevitable questions directed to *Hansard* reporters: "Which system is fastest? Which do you recommend?"

Put plainly, the results achieved with the system chosen, be it Pitman, Gregg, or Stenotype, depend on the efforts of the individual student, who would be advised to practice, in Pitman, the obligatory shading to distinguish between light and dark strokes, and in Gregg to practice endless circles and ellipses, until repetition produces the desired dexterity in wrist and fingers. Until the two hundreds words a minute barrier has been broken, no attempt should be made to incorporate personalized shortcuts.

The Thompsons

THROUGHOUT its history, shorthand has had an attraction for various families, extending over a number of generations. The Duployé reporting brothers in Paris have their Canadian counterparts, perhaps most notably in recent years the Hubbard family of Ottawa, the Buskards of Brantford, and the Price family of Thunder Bay. None, however, have risen higher than the Thompsons of Nova Scotia.

John Sparrow Thompson was born in Waterford, Ireland, in 1795. Like many another of his generation, his struggle to acquire an education was dedicated and difficult. The book learning he pursued with relentless diligence as a youth lifted him from being a bootmaker to a career as a schoolteacher, newspaper correspondent, parliamentary reporter, friend and confidant of Joseph Howe, poet, littérateur, publisher, and the recipient throughout his life of the respect and, indeed, veneration of all who knew him.

When and where Thompson first learned shorthand is unknown. Between 1810 and 1820, some twenty-two shorthand books, covering almost as many systems, were published. The most widely used of the era was the Gurney system, first issued in 1750, although rivalled by Samuel Taylor's shorthand. But whichever system he wrote, Thompson mastered it and used it skilfully in the service of his adopted country.

As a young man, Thompson spent some time in London before deciding to emigrate to Nova Scotia. The date of his arrival in Halifax is uncertain, but a reference made by Howe in 1838 to their close association of twelve years, indicates that he had established himself there by the middle of the 1820s. He married, became a schoolteacher, and began to contribute to various periodicals. His practise of shorthand supplemented his earnings from teaching, a necessity in days before the establishment of the public school system, and by the early 1830s he was much in demand as a shorthand reporter.

In 1835 a libel trial of lasting consequence for both Nova Scotia and Canada took place: *the King* vs. *Joseph Howe*. This work is not concerned with the political aftermath. It merely places on record that the shorthand reporter at the trial was J. S. Thompson, then in his fortieth year and entering a period of activity that paralleled Howe's now full-hearted commitment to the attainment of responsible government.

Naturally, Thompson was labelled a radical, then a term of opprobrium, but nowadays easily equated with reformer. A friend, J.A. Bell, described him in this period as follows:

> He was something more than a liberal; he was a radical out and out. Not however, a hater of England or British institutions. On the contrary, I never knew a man who was a more sincere admirer of both. But he was a lover of equal rights, a hater of class privileges and had about him a strong sense of independence which scorned anything like sycophancy.*

From 1836 to 1838, Thompson conducted the *Acadian Recorder*, and something of the style of the man emerges from his stated proposal "to collect news, without views." He was not cast for commerce, though, and at the end of that time was glad to go to work for Howe, reporting the debates in the House of Assembly for the *Novascotian*.

Howe valued Thompson's judgment highly. As Hendry tells us:

> . . . Howe, though first and foremost and beyond everything else a politician, had a corner in his heart for letters and the Muses, and in John S. Thompson found a kindred spirit. Howe rarely wrote anything that he deemed of any consequence, especially in verse, that was not submitted to Thompson, such confidence had he in the latter's taste and critical judgment. The confidence was not misplaced for Thompson was both an honest and competent critic.

---

*W.A. Hendry in an unpublished ms., Thompson Papers, Public Archives of Canada, 001808.

He would not spare a false quantity, a defective metaphor, a weak expletive or a coarse allusion, to please his friend, Mr Howe, or anybody else.

Evidence of Howe's trust is amply demonstrated in the following report taken from the *Novascotian*. It deals with the death of another Thompson, many years later:

> When the day came that Howe was obliged to lay down the editorial pen for a time . . . he placed Thompson in the vacant editorial chair, and in the open and frank manner so characteristic of Howe, he used these emphatic words—genuine words which ring out an encomium such as any literary man might well covet:—"As a parliamentary reporter and a writer of taste and genius, Thompson has few equals and no superior in this Province."

Thompson continued to serve Nova Scotia well until his death on 2 October 1867, at the age of seventy-two. He became Queen's Printer, and later was connected with the Post Office. Of his wife, the former Miss Pottinger, little is known except that she came from the Orkneys, but their household was a happy one, blessed with four daughters and three sons, one of the latter becoming, in 1892, the fourth Prime Minister of Canada.

The *Novascotian* had more to say about John Sparrow Thompson:

> Had he been of an aggressive disposition, instead of being the most unselfish of men, and had he been inspired with an ambition to step over the heads of his fellows, doubtless he could have reached a high place of distinction in the public eye, and thus had his name written in more indelible letters in the page of history, but he preferred to live in retirement, and to cultivate his literary tastes in the quiet of his own fireside. He did his work for his adopted country, none the less effectively however; and he gave to Canada, equipped with high intellectual attainments, prepared as from the hands of a skilled workman, a son who attained the highest position of trust . . .

In appearance John Sparrow Thompson's son was stern, upright and clean-shaven. He had a sense of responsibility that permeated both his public and private lives. And yet there was a generosity of character that could not resist appeals for aid, no matter what their source.

Sir John S. D. Thompson was born in Halifax on 10 November 1844, when his father was forty-nine. Fortunately, a wealth of family correspondence included with the Thompson Papers in the Public Archives of Canada reveals the inner human being and goes far to explain his success in the various callings to which he devoted his talents.

Visitors to the House of Commons in Ottawa can see his portrait on the wall south of the Foyer to the Chamber, close to that of Sir John A. Macdonald, his sponsor, mentor and far-seeing associate.

There can be little question that the father bequeathed to his son many of his own traits. In childhood, there was the emphasis on education as the key to improvement and advancement. His own experience as a teacher was helpful in channeling the young boy's natural curiosity, and he saw to it that his son benefited fully from study during his years in the public school system, something he himself had not experienced. But it was the home, the family in which he grew up, that most influenced the development of Thompson's character and conscience.

The twenty-three years he spent at home, before the death of his father in 1867, were a solid foundation on which to build, and it is little wonder that in later years, despite worldly successes, Thompson's greatest pride was taken in his own family, his wife and children. His absences from home sorely tried him. The almost daily correspondence between wife and husband, when his duties took him to Ottawa, is ample evidence of the sense of loss each felt in the other's absence.

At fifteen, Thompson was articled as a law student. W. J. Healy, writing in Ottawa in 1891, relates that "he had already [1859] made himself a skilled stenographer."* When we recall the tribute paid to his father as a parliamentary reporter, there is no need to wonder how he became a skilled shorthand writer at such an early age.

---

*W.J. Healy, "Sir John Thompson" in Louis H. Taché (ed.), *Men of the Day: A Canadian Portrait Gallery*, Vol. I (Ottawa: Louis H. Taché, 1890).

Sir John S. Thompson, age 46

Like father, like son. The younger Thompson soon turned to reporting the parliamentary debates in the Nova Scotia House of Assembly. The reporter-in-chief at the time was John George Bourinot, who, in submitting his report of the debates in 1866, chose to comment, "I also beg to acknowledge the excellence of the work done by my assistant, Mr John S. D. Thompson."

In 1867, Bourinot left Halifax for Ottawa. Thompson succeeded him as reporter-in-chief, and continued to report the legislature's debates for the following four sessions.

Thompson had been called to the Bar in 1865, when he was twenty-one years old, so he was carrying out both his legal duties and parliamentary reporting duties at the same time. Since the Assembly's sessions lasted just two to three months, the practice could be understood.

These years were also to give Canadians one of the most penetrating glimpses into the lives of young people in Halifax some one hundred and ten or more years ago.

The story is a simple one. John S. D. Thompson went a-courting. The object of his affection was a Miss Annie Affleck, a native Haligonian, whose father was a sea captain. The courtship was an ardent one. And it was lengthy. In those times convention allowed the suitor to call on his beloved, at home. Thompson called, and called. For over three years he wooed the sea captain's daughter, and during that time he taught her French and shorthand.

Annie recorded it all in her diary, and that diary, at least a portion of it for 1867, now reposes in the Public Archives of Canada. It is a quaintly interesting document. Written on lined, blue paper, possibly taken from an exercise book, it tells of talks and walks, shows the tempo of her days, and mentions Thompson in almost every entry.

Curiously, Annie speaks of her suitor simply as Thompson. Time and again there appear such entries as the following for 29 November 1867 and succeeding days:

"Thompson in and we spent the evening talking." Saturday, November 30th: "Thompson in and spent the evening. We only kind of talked." Sunday, December 1st, 1867: "—writing some

shorthand until about 9 o'clock. Then Thompson in for a time."
Tuesday, January 3rd: "Thompson in this evening. I wrote some
shorthand and we talked. I wonder how long my fit of independence
is going to last." Monday, December 23rd: "Thompson in about 9
o'clock. Spent the evening talking and reading some French."
Tuesday, December 24th: "Christmas Eve. Kind of busy all day.
Day fine but cold. Over to confession this morning. Reading for a
little while and Thompson in about 9 o'clock. We spent the evening
very quietly sitting by the fire. How different from other Christmas
Eves I feel this one, a kind of quiet content that at one time . . . I
thought I could never feel."

The entry for Christmas is rather lengthy, but worth quoting for
the serenity it displays:

Wednesday, December 25—and as a matter of course Christmas.
Could not sleep through the night. Up and down to 6 o'clock mass.
Pleasant going down but cold and bright coming home. Received
Holy Communion. Feeling not very well after I came home, laid
down until about 2 o'clock. T. in and staid [sic] a little while this
afternoon, also this evening. We sat and chatted the evening away.
So ends this Christmas. It is passed and gone, and with it the year is
nearly gone too. A few days more and it will have passed away . . .
and part of our life with it.

And for the last day of 1867 Annie could confide to her dairy:

I am happier this night than I have ever been before on the
threshold of another year . . . I used to look forward and expect.
Now I can close my log, say good night to the old year and shake
hands with the new. That old restless longing has left me and I am
content to do the little that comes in my way, to do without many
things, to expect nothing . . .

To study shorthand and another language, and both to make
and keep her own diary, bespoke the determination and will of the
future Lady Thompson, who bore eight children, and whose
counsel was instrumental in sending her husband into Dominion
politics, something not even the importuning of Sir John A.
Macdonald was able to accomplish.

Some may wonder what all this reference to Thompson's courtship has to do with the history of *Hansard* in Canada. The answer lies in Miss Affleck's log. Day after day she recorded her innermost thoughts in meticulously scripted shorthand. And there may be reason to believe that some of the shorthand entries were made by Thompson himself. Certainly a comparison of his own shorthand with a number of pages in the diary, could reasonably indicate they were written by the same hand. In sum, Affleck was an embryo Canadian female Pepys, but to date no one in Ottawa has succeeded in deciphering the secret symbols of the winged art used by either Thompson or his lady.*

In 1877, seven years after his marriage, and having built up a successful law practice, John S. D. Thompson successfully ran in a by-election in Antigonish, and joined the Tory opposition in the provincial House of Assembly. A year later the Liberal government was defeated in a general election, and Thompson became Attorney-General in the incoming administration. This narrative is not concerned with his successes and failures in politics, save to mention that on the return of the Liberals to power in 1882, Thompson was appointed a judge of the Supreme Court of Nova Scotia, which position he held for three years, before entering federal politics in 1885 and immediately becoming Minister of Justice of the Dominion of Canada.

A newspaper article of that time gave the following picture of the emerging Nova Scotian:

> Starting like nearly all young men of his time, as a follower of Howe in the ante-Confederation period, more from personal fondness perhaps than from a profound conviction, he gladly acquiesced in the acceptance by Howe, in 1867, of the "better terms" which by the wise determination of Sir John Macdonald were made the sign and seal of Imperial as well as of Canadian politics. Since 1869 he has been a most faithful, high-minded, unselfish and respected advocate of the policy of the great chief of the Liberal-Conservative

---

*In a footnote to his paper, "John Thompson Goes to Ottawa, 1885," *The Dalhousie Review*, Winter 1977-78, P.B. Waite suggests that it was a variation of Gurney's shorthand. The historian or sleuth who wishes to pursue the subject would do well to inspect the original in Volume 289 of the Thompson Papers in the Public Archives of Canada.

Party of Canada. As a lawyer his success has been remarkable. He has the faculty of initiative, and is really "learned in the law." As an orator his style is usually subdued but effective, and in due season on proper provocation he can exercise a power of declamation quite remarkable in one who is not effusive in manner. His gift of accomplished sarcasm has been the secret terror of a good many bumptious gentlemen . . .

Thompson was knighted in 1885, became Prime Minister of Canada on 5 December 1892, and died during a visit to Windsor Castle on 12 December 1894. He was but fifty years of age.

The above is a sample of the shorthand written by Sir John Thompson, Canada's fourth Prime Minister, and a former Hansard *reporter, when presiding over proceedings as a member of the Supreme Court of Nova Scotia, on 14 July, 1883.*

John George Bourinot

T HERE are two outstanding authorities on parliamentary procedure in Canada, Bourinot and Beauchesne. John George
Bourinot's work was the earlier of the two and, in the absence of
any benchmark, was widely received with acclaim. He had intel-
lectual brilliance and the talent of an all-engaging industriousness
which he devoted without stint to the service of his country.

Today a bronze bust of Bourinot can be seen in the Clerk's office
in the Canadian House of Commons. Early photographs of the
Parliament in session give prominence to Bourinot sitting at the
Table of the House. His papers, articles, even scrapbooks, are
frequently consulted by the student and historian. His fame rests
secure. But the one work for which he was most lauded, the
capstone of his career, Bourinot's *Parliamentary Procedure and
Practice*, is now largely neglected. Beauchesne has taken pre-
eminence, with secondary dependence falling on Westminster's
Erskine May, despite the many differences in practice between the
English and Canadian institutions.

Bourinot was first and foremost a *Hansard* man. A Nova Scotian,
who served his parliamentary reporting apprenticeship in the
province's House of Assembly, he became in 1870 the first officially
appointed "Short-hand Writer to the Senate." He held this position until 1873, when he transferred to the Lower House, surely
one of the very few in Canadian parliamentary history to make the
journey between both Houses in reverse.

Bourinot was born in Sydney, Cape Breton, on 24 October 1837,
the year of Mackenzie's abortive uprising in Upper Canada. His
father, Lt. Colonel John Bourinot, a native of Jersey in the Channel
Islands and a Huguenot of Norman ancestry, became Vice-consul

Sir John George Bourinot

for France during his residence of fifty years in Sydney, and from 1859 until Confederation represented Cape Breton in the House of Assembly.

The boy grew to manhood in comfortable circumstances:

> Sydney is one of the chief resorts of the French North Atlantic squadron, and there is generally a French man-of-war in the harbour in summer. Near the water's edge is the large white Bourinot Mansion, long the home of Senator Bourinot, French Vice-consul, and containing numerous and interesting mementoes of Sydney's visits from the French Navy.*

The father's hospitality was a by-word throughout the province, and the son's social graces and early acquaintance with notable visitors were to stand him in good stead in the advancement of his career.

Bourinot received his early education from a tutor, the Rev. W. Y. Porter, and his mental prowess was soon to become evident. He was sent to Trinity College in Toronto, where he won a number of scholarships. It is said he was so accomplished in various fields that the choice of a vocation was difficult to make. After considering the church and the law, he settled on journalism. It is not known under what circumstances he acquired a knowledge of and facility in shorthand, but he was soon occupied in reporting the debates in the House of Assembly.

In 1860, at twenty-three, he became the founder and editor of the Halifax *Reporter*. No doubt his family connections assisted him in undertaking this venture at such an early age. Dr George Stewart, of Quebec, has written that the new newspaper quickly gained a reputation "for the brilliancy and independence of its editorials, and the faithfulness of its parliamentary reports."†

In the following year, Bourinot accepted the post of chief of the staff reporting the House of Assembly debates, a position he held

---

*Madge Macbeth, "A Great Canadian: Sir John Bourinot," *The Dalhousie Review*, Vol. XXXIV (Summer 1954), 173-80.

†In a chapter on Bourinot in *Men of the Day: A Canadian Portrait Gallery*, op. cit., p. 202.

for the next six years. During this period he was to gain the friendship of Joseph Howe, Charles Tupper, and others prominent in the political life of the Maritime provinces.

J. S. Martell brings into question the fullness of the reports of the provincial debates, noting that in 1860 John S. Thompson (presumably Thompson senior) "agreed to employ a staff of reporters who would enable him to give 'somewhat condensed, but fair reports'" of the proceedings, and mentioning that Bourinot "who carried on from 1864 to Confederation engaged himself to furnish 150 copies of 'a pamphlet containing the reports as they appear in the papers' and 'an index on all the subjects discussed in the House.'"*

With Confederation, the name of Bourinot's father, John, appeared in the Proclamation of Confederation issued by Queen Victoria, one of the first men appointed a member of the Senate of Canada. As has already been said, Bourinot himself became the first officially appointed "Short-hand Writer to the Senate," where he continued to do the type of work he had previously undertaken for his own province. This certainly was the first Senate father and son phenomenon, and it was not to be the last.

In 1873 the son deserted the Senate for the more lively life of the Commons, where he became the second clerk assistant. Six years later he was appointed first clerk assistant, and on 18 December 1880 became the Clerk of the House of Commons. And so it came to pass that the former Nova Scotian *Hansard* reporter assumed administrative control of the first official *Hansard* staff of the House of Commons of Canada.

For the next twenty-two years, until his death, following a long illness, on 13 October 1902, at the age of sixty-five years, Bourinot's industry, indefatigability and experience were employed fully, both in the service of Parliament and of literature, art and science.

---

*"Early Parliamentary Reporting in Nova Scotia 1817-1837," *The Canadian Historical Review*, Vol. XXI (1940), 385.

The reference to an index prompts a brief mention of the excellent work done by Mrs Nonnie Murray of the Nova Scotia *Hansard* staff, in indexing the debates during the 1970s. Her talk on the subject of indexing parliamentary debates, given to a meeting of the Canadian Hansard Association in Halifax in 1976, was a uniquely direct and simple explanation of this complicated procedure.

In Parliament, his knowledge of procedure was unparalleled; outside Parliament, his successes were many and varied. However, it cannot be said that he was unquestioningly accepted as the literary figure nonpareil. Appointed secretary of the Royal Society of Canada by the Marquis of Lorne, Canada's fourth Governor-General, he was guilty of allowing some slipshod work to escape his pen, and came in for a roasting from one of the more peculiar figures to rise to prominence in the political life of the country.

In a pamphlet issued by Nicholas Flood Davin at Ottawa, in 1882, Bourinot was denounced as "a literary fraud." Vivisecting his prose without mercy, Flood Davin railed at Bourinot's unfortunate effusion, accusing him of having "the grammatical elegance of a scullion."

> I cannot conclude without congratulating the Government on having passed a Civil Service Reform Bill, which requires some test to be applied to those seeking admission to the Service. Never again, I hope, will a man so illiterate as Mr Bourinot, a man who could not at this moment pass an examination for a third class clerkship, climb or crawl to the position of "*the* Clerk of the Canadian House of Commons." It is not creditable to Canada. It is not creditable to the House of Commons. It is not creditable to the Civil Service.*

The Governor-General was not amused, and Bourinot remained secretary of the society. Whether Davin's outburst was responsible for it or not, few other Clerks of the Canadian House of Commons ventured into print, the standard work presently most quoted being Beauchesne's *Parliamentary Rules and Forms*, written by Dr Arthur Beauchesne when occupying that position in 1922. Revised by the author through four editions until 1958, it underwent further revision and updating in 1978, a most necessary undertaking in view of the many procedural changes sanctioned by Parliament in the intervening years.

Sir John George Bourinot was a trail-blazer from Nova Scotia. Howe and Tupper and Thompson, all friends, all of the same

*N.F. Davin, *The Secretary of the Royal Society of Canada, A Literary Fraud* (Ottawa: 1882), p. 20.

*The House of Commons Chamber near the turn of the century.
Sir Wilfrid Laurier, Prime Minister, is sitting next to a vacant seat; Sir J.G. Bourinot, Clerk, sits at the head of the Table.*

political bent, were to serve in the House of Commons with him.*
There was delicious irony in the spectacle of two former *Hansard*
reporters, Bourinot and Thompson, sitting in the Chamber within
a few feet of each other, the Clerk of the House of Commons, and
the Prime Minister of Canada. Who knows what *Hansard* has yet
to offer the nation?

---

*A plaque commemorating the first reporting of parliamentary debates in Canada, and
honouring Thompson and Bourinot, was unveiled at Province House, Halifax, on 26 August
1976 by Premier Gerald Regan.

Appendix One

HANSARD ROLL OF HONOUR
HOUSE OF COMMONS
CANADA
1880–1980

ABBOTT, Stephen A.	1880–1912
ALLEN, Una	1969–
ARCHAMBAULT, Fernand	1961–1976
BAKER, Douglas A.	1960–
BENOIT, Hector	1939–1944
BENSON, A.B.	1952–1954
BERRYMAN, Frederick	1919–1932
BIRD, P.	1962–1963
BLAIR, Joan C.	1957–1959
BLUE, Charles Steedman	1912–1919
BRADLEY, George B.	1880–1899
BUSKARD, W. Warren	1926–1969
BUTT, Donald R.	1944–1961
CAMPBELL, Alexander Colin	1894–1926
CLINTON, William J.	1948–1964
COGHILL, Donald H.	1966–1978
DESJARDINS, Alphonse	1892–1918
DEVOST, Jean-Claude	1971–1975
DICKSON, W.H.	1918–1930

DOCHERTY, C.G.	1953-1954
DUGGAN, E. Joseph	1880-1912
DUNBAR, Robert C.	1903-1921
DYER, Joseph	1964-
EMPRINGHAM, Charles L.	1931-1969
EYVEL, George	1880-1888
FEATHERSTON, Edward L.	1930-1961
FISHER, Charles J.	1957-
FRENETTE, Paul	1949-1966
GABARD, Marcel	1918-1938
GALBRAITH, Frederick W.S.	1912-1949
GRANDMAISON, A.	1960-1962
GUERTIN, Lucien R.	1951-1973
HORTON, Albert	1880-1916
HUBBARD, Thomas Stephen	1919-1957
JOHNSTON, M.F.	1921-1930
LACOMBE, Honorius	1968-
LANGLOIS, R.	1952-1962
LECOMPTE, Marie-Paule	1979-
LUMSDEN, John A.	1883-1884
LUSK, Leslie	1969-
MACKAY, J. Henri	1921-1949
MAILLE, Bernadette	1975-
MARCEAU, F.R.	1880-1892
MARCEAU, J.O.	1883-1921
MORAND, Robert	1975-
MORRISON, Brenda	1977-
NAUBERT, André	1949-1967
OBORNE, Lilian Bolduc-	1975-

OLIVER, Harold E.	1914-1948
OWENS, Thomas Patrick	1888-1921
PARSONS, Peter W.	1959-
PLAYLE, George H.	1932-1944
POTVIN, Brian	1977-
PRICE, Newell L.	1949-1974
RICHARDSON, Thomas Jno.	1884-1894
ROBERTSON, John G.	1949-1977
ROBINSON, Noel	1955-1957
ST. JEAN, Gaston	1962-
SAVARD, Pierre	1968-
SHELTON, Percy H.	1936-1948
SIMPSON, George	1899-1936
SPITZER, Andrew S.	1966-1977
STRASZAK, Ita	1966-
TREMAINE, Ronald	1978-
WARD, John	1962-
WATSON, Isaac	1880-1883
WATTRIPOINT, Danielle	1963-1968
WHITE, Roger	1956-1963
YOUNG, Earl Courtney	1912-1952

Appendix Two

The following is a report of a committee of the House of Assembly, dated 17 February 1830, on conditions in York jail. The committee was appointed following receipt of a petition from certain prisoners. By this time Collins had been released, and no claim can be made that the committee was influenced by his experience.

In the cells below the ground floor, your committee found three female lunatics confined, one of them from England, and who is understood to be the mother of a family, who became deranged on her husband leaving her; another from Ireland, a young woman, and the third a native of Canada. It was stated by the Jailor that they have as wholesome and nutricious [*sic*] food as himself and family, and there is a stove in the dungeon; but they are lodged in locked up cribs, on straw, two in one crib, and the other by herself; one of them contrived to set fire to the jail some time ago, but it was providentially discovered in time to save the building, by cutting down a door that was in flames. A gentleman confined for debt complained that the smell from the dungeon in which these poor lunatics are confined, which below the room was almost insupportable, and that their incessant howlings and groans were annoying in the extreme. The smell is certainly most disagreeable, and confinement in such a noisome place will be likely to aggravate the disorder; who, were they taken to a particular ward in the Hospital, and the usual restraints put upon their persons (of strait waistcoats), and gently treated, might either wholly recover their reason, or at least become convalescent. Their confinement is severe beyond that of the most hardened criminal, although their situation entitles them to a double portion of the favourable regard of all in whom the blessing of reason has been bestowed.

Your Committee found 25 persons in this prison, twelve criminals on the ground floor, one criminal sick upstairs, one vagrant,
the three lunatics above mentioned, and nine debtors.

Thomas McMahon, a criminal, complained that he had only a
jail allowance of three half pence worth, or one pound of bread,
and water; that soap, sufficient to keep the prisoners clean, was not
given; that some of the prisoners are several weeks together, without changes of linen; that he had enough of bed clothes, but that
they had not been washed, he believed, for six or eight months. The
smell of his dungeon was very noisome.

John Thompson, under a respite from a sentence of death, &
who is one of the petitioners, had, since the date of the petition,
been allowed six pence per day, by order of the Bank directors. In a
letter to one of the members of your Committee, he renews his
complaint concerning the quality of the food allowed him. All the
other prisoners in this ward complain of the scantiness of the jail
allowance, only three half pence worth of bread per diem. Your
Committee think that although a place of imprisonment is not intended to be a place of comfort, it should not be a place of starva-
tion. This allowance is too small; it is less, your Committee understand, than the allowance in other Districts, and is especially hard
towards those who have no friends to help them. The request of the
prisoners is six pence a day, or its value in bread.

Some of the prisoners are mechanics, but they are not at work.
About a dozen of them are allowed to be together in the day time,
in the same ward. This is a pernicious, and in this province, an
unnecessary practice. For instance, your Committee saw the apprentice of a tradesman in town, in company with persons charged
with murder, and criminals of the very worst description—among
them the person respited under sentence of death. The apprentice
was incarcerated for having refused to attend his master's work;
and the company into which the verdict of the Magistrates has
thrown him will not be likely to improve either his manners or his
morals. A criminal ward upstairs being empty, this classification of
offenders deserves from your Committee the more severe reprobation.

The cell of James McMahon, and that of John Wilson, stink so
as scarcely to be fit to breathe in. The jail itself is ill constructed;

and the jail privy being stopped up adds to the unwholesomeness of the atmosphere, in a degree, that even in winter, is almost intolerable. The water closets ought to be taken away, and a proper substitute provided; the chloride of lime, or some other salt ought to be used from time to time, to purify the apartments, and such other means used as would render a residence within these walls less grievous.

The debtors are, with one exception, all on the upper floor, apart from the other prisoners. Three of them are confined on mesne process, issued out of the King's Bench, and one on mesne process issued out of the District Court. These are allowed no support from their creditors, and some of them say they are entirely without the means of subsistance. James Colquhoun is in jail for a debt of three pounds; the creditor has forgiven the debt, but the lawyer has not thought proper to forgive his fees. Colquhoun subsists entirely on the humanity of the jailor and other debtors. One Murphy told your Committee that he had nothing to eat and that both Colquhoun and himself had been for days together, without tasting a morsel.

There are six debtors confined on executions issued out of the Court of King's Bench.

One debtor is in jail, together with his wife, and a family of five children.

Your Committee observed only one person at work; he was a shoemaker.

Your Committee would recommend advising His Excellency the Lieutenant Governor, requesting the interference of Government on behalf of these prisoners.

A petition to the quarter Sessions, was not, it appears, productive of any good effects.

The signature to the report is that of W. L. Mackenzie, Committee chairman. It was presented to the House of Assembly on 28 February 1830. To the surprise of nobody in Parliament, no action was taken on it.

Bibliography

PRIMARY SOURCES

Newspapers
Canadian Freeman 1825-1834
Colonial Advocate
Gazette, Montreal
Globe, Toronto
The Newry Magazine 1815
The Ulster Magazine 1830
The Ulster Recorder 1815
The Ulster Register 1816-1817
Upper Canada Gazette
Vindicator & Canadian Advertiser
York Observer

Parliamentary Debates
The Debates of the House of Commons 1875-1980
The Debates of the Senate of Canada (various)
Journals of the House of Assembly 1829, 1830, 1831

Unpublished Manuscripts
Sir John S. Thompson Papers (Public Archives of Canada)
Hendry, W.A. "An Outline of the Life of J.S. Thompson." Unpublished MS (Public Archives of Canada)
Upper Canada Sundries, Land Petitions, State Papers, Civil Secretary's Correspondence, Manuscript Journals of the Executive Council (Public Archives of Canada)
Bengough, Thomas. "A History of the Ontario Court Reporting Staff." Unpublished MS, 1931.

Campbell, A.C. "The Canadian Hansard." Unpublished MS, 1932.

Various Government Publications and Reports
Final Report on the Constitution of Canada by the Special Committee of the Senate and House of Commons. Ottawa: Queen's Printer, 1972.

Our Parliamentary Heritage by Archives of Ontario. Toronto: Ministry of Culture and Recreation, 1967.

A Time to Speak—The Views of the Public by the Task Force on Canadian Unity. Ottawa: Queen's Printers, 1979.

SECONDARY SOURCES

Ackroyd, P.R. and C.F. Evans. *The Cambridge History of the Bible*. Cambridge: Cambridge University Press, 1970.

Aspinall, A. *Politics and the Press 1780-1850*. London: Home & Van Thal Ltd, 1949.

Baker, Alfred. *The Life of Sir Isaac Pitman*, centenary edition. London: Sir Isaac Pitman & Sons Ltd, 1913.

Baldwin, R.M. and J. Baldwin. *The Baldwins and the Great Experiment*. Toronto: Longmans, 1969.

Bovey, Wilfrid. *The French Canadians Today*. Abridged by George Buxton. Harmondsworth: Penguin Books, 1942.

Brother Alfred, Rev. "Francis Collins—First Catholic Journalist in Upper Canada," in *Canadian Catholic Historical Association Report 1938-39*, pp. 51-66.

Burrell, Martin. *Betwixt Heaven and Charing Cross*. Toronto: The Macmillan Company of Canada Limited, 1928.

Buskard, W. Warren. *Parliamentary Reporting in Canada*. New Delhi: Pitman Shorthand School, 1961.

Butler, E.H. *The Story of British Shorthand*. London: Sir Isaac Pitman & Sons Ltd, 1951.

Clinton, W.J. "Xanthates," in *The Chartered Shorthand Reporter*, March 1945.

Cronin, P.F. "Early Catholic Journalism in Canada," in *Canadian Catholic Historical Association Report 1935-36.*

Davin, Nicholas Flood. *The Irishman in Canada.* Toronto: 1877.

——————. *The Secretary of the Royal Society of Canada, A Literary Fraud.* Ottawa: 1882.

Dent, John Charles. *The Story of the Upper Canadian Rebellion.* Toronto: The Carswell Company Ltd, 1899.

——————. *The Upper Canadian Rebellion.* Toronto: C. Blackett Robinson, 1885.

Doubourdieu, Rev. J. *Statistical Survey of the County of Down.* Dublin: Graisberry and Campbell, 1802.

Firth, Edith G. *The Town of York 1815-1834.* Toronto: The Champlain Society, 1966.

Flynn, Louis J. *Built on a Rock.* The Roman Catholic Archdiocese of Kingston, 1976.

Fraser, Alexander. *The Last Laird of MacNab.* Toronto: Imrie, Graham & Company, 1889.

Gard, Anson A. *Pioneers of the Upper Ottawa.* Ottawa: Emerson Press, 1907.

Hayes, John F. *The Nation Builders.* Toronto: The Copp Clark Publishing Company, 1968.

Healy, W.J. "Sir John Thompson," in Louis H. Taché (ed.) *Men of the Day: A Canadian Portrait Gallery.* Ottawa: Louis H. Taché, 1890.

Inglis, Brian. *The Freedom of the Press in Ireland 1784-1841.* London: Faber and Faber, 1954.

James, Robert Rhodes. *An Introduction to the House of Commons.* London: Collins, 1961.

Kesterton, W.H. *A History of Journalism in Canada.* Toronto: McClelland and Stewart Limited, 1967.

Macbeth, Madge. "A Great Canadian: Sir John Bourinot." *The Dalhousie Review,* Vol. XXXIV (Summer 1954), 173-80.

Martell, J.S. "Early Parliamentary Reporting in Nova Scotia 1817-1837." *The Canadian Historical Review,* Vol. XXI (1940).

——————. "The Press of the Maritime Provinces in the 1830s." *The Canadian Historical Review,* Vol. XIX (1938), 24-59.

McGee, Thomas D'Arcy. *Historical Sketches of O'Connell and Friends.* Boston: Donahoe and Rohan, 1845.

McGiffin, J. Stuart. *The Story of the Professional Institute 1920-1945.* Ottawa: The Professional Institute of the Public Service of Canada, 1945.

McLean, Mary. "Early Parliamentary Reporting in Upper Canada." *The Canadian Historical Review,* Vol. XX (1939), 378-91.

Merritt, J.P. *Hon. W.H. Merritt, M.P.* St Catharine's: S. Leavenworth, 1875.

Middleton, J.E. *The Municipality of Toronto—A History.* Toronto: The Dominion Publishing Company, 1923.

Middleton, J.E. and Fred Landon. *The Province of Ontario—A History.* Toronto: The Dominion Publishing Company, 1927.

Mitchel, John. *History of Ireland.* Glasgow: Cameron, Ferguson & Company, n.d.

Mullally, Emmet J. "Dr Daniel Tracey, A Pioneer Worker for Responsible Government in Canada," in *Canadian Catholic Historical Association Report, 1934-35.*

Mulvany, C. Pelham. *Toronto: Past and Present.* Toronto: W.E. Caiger, 1884.

Nish, Elizabeth. *Debates of the Legislative Assembly of Upper Canada 1841-1867.* Vol. I. Reprinted by the Centre d'Etude du Quebec and the Centre de recherche en histoire économique du Canada français.

O'Brien, Barry. *The Life of Lord Russell of Killowen.* London: Thomas Nelson & Sons, n.d.

Pilling, J.S. *Bibliography of the Chinookan Languages.* Washington: Smithsonian Institution, 1893.

Rankin, D.J. Rev. *A History of the County of Antigonish, Nova Scotia.* Toronto: The Macmillan Company of Canada Limited, 1929.

Read, D.B. *The Lieutenant-Governors of Upper Canada and Ontario 1792-1899.* Toronto: William Briggs, 1900.

Rouillard, H. *Pioneers in Adult Education in Canada.* Toronto: Nelson, 1964.

Scadding, Henry. *Toronto of Old: Collections and Recollections.* Toronto: Adam, Stevenson & Company, 1873.

Scott, George. *Reporter Anonymous, The Story of the Press Association.* London: Hutchinson, 1968.

Shelley, Percy Bysshe. *An Address to the Irish People.* Dublin: 1812.

Smith, Edward. *William Cobbett.* 2 vols. London: Sampson, Low, Marston, Searle & Rivington, 1878.

Stewart, George. "John George Bourinot," in Louis H. Taché (ed.) *Men of the Day: A Canadian Portrait Gallery.* Ottawa: Louis H. Taché, 1890.

Swettenham, John and David Dealy. *Serving the State—A History of The Professional Institute of the Public Service of Canada 1920-1970.* Ottawa: Le Droit, 1970.

Talbot, Edward Allen. *Five Years' Residence in the Canadas.* London: Longman, Hurst, Rees, Orme, Brown and Greene, 1824.

Talman, J.J. "The Newspapers of Upper Canada a Century Ago." *The Canadian Historical Review,* Vol. XIX (1938).

Taylor, Samuel. *An Essay Intended to Establish a Standard for an Universal System of Stenography or Short Hand Writing.* London: J. Bell, Bookseller, Strand, 1786.

——————. *Taylor's Universal System of Shorthand Writing.* 4th edition. London: 1807.

Thompson, Samuel. *Reminiscences of a Canadian Pioneer.* Toronto: Hunter, Rose & Company, 1884.

Waite, P.B. (ed.). *House of Commons Debates 1867-68.* Ottawa: Queen's Printer, 1967.

——————. "John Thompson Goes to Ottawa, 1885," *The Dalhousie Review,* (Winter 1977/78), 605-18.

Wallace, W. Stewart. *The Family Compact—A Chronicle of the Rebellion in Upper Canada.* Toronto: Glasgow, Brook and Company, 1915.

——————. "The Periodical Literature of Upper Canada," in *The Canadian Historical Review,* Vol. XII (1931)

Ward, John. "Hansard in the Parliament of Canada: Past—Present —Future," in *Hansard Association Report, 1976.*

Ward, John Manning. *Colonial Self-Government: The British Experience 1759-1856.* Toronto: University of Toronto Press, 1976.

Yeigh, Frank. *Ontario's Parliament Buildings.* Toronto: Williamson Book Company, 1893.

Young, Earl C. "Hansard." A nationwide broadcast in Canada, November 1944.

Index

Page numbers in **bold** indicate illustrations.